HOME GAME

An Accidental Guide to Fatherhood

MICHAEL LEWIS

Photographs by Tabitha Soren

PENGUIN BOOKS

PENGUIN BOOKS

Published by the Penguin Group
Penguin Books Ltd, 80 Strand, London WC2R 0RL, England
Penguin Group (USA) Inc., 375 Hudson Street, New York, New York 10014, USA
Penguin Group (Canada), 90 Eglinton Avenue East, Suite 700, Toronto, Ontario, Canada M4P 2Y3
(a division of Pearson Penguin Canada Inc.)
Penguin Ireland, 25 St Stephen's Green, Dublin 2, Ireland (a division of Penguin Books Ltd)
Penguin Group (Australia), 250 Camberwell Road, Camberwell, Victoria 3124, Australia
(a division of Pearson Australia Group Pty Ltd)
Penguin Books India Pvt Ltd, 11 Community Centre, Panchsheel Park, New Delhi – 110 017, India
Penguin Group (NZ), 67 Apollo Drive, Rosedale, North Shore 0632, New Zealand
(a division of Pearson New Zealand Ltd)
Penguin Books (South Africa) (Pty) Ltd, 24 Sturdee Avenue, Rosebank,
Johannesburg 2196, South Africa

Penguin Books Ltd, Registered Offices: 80 Strand, London WC2R 0RL, England

www.penguin.com

First published in the United States of America by W. W. Norton & Co. 2009
First published in Great Britain by Penguin Books 2009

010

Copyright © Michael Lewis, 2009
Photographs copyright © Tabitha Soren, 2009
All rights reserved

The moral right of the author has been asserted

Printed in England by Clays Ltd, Elcograf S.p.A.

978-0-141-04319-7

www.greenpenguin.co.uk

MIX
Paper from
responsible sources
FSC
www.fsc.org   FSC® C018179

Penguin Books is committed to a sustainable
future for our business, our readers and our planet.
This book is made from Forest Stewardship
Council™ certified paper.

FOR QUINN & DIXIE & WALKER

If you don't want to see it in print, don't do it.

CONTENTS

INTRODUCTION

I INHERITED FROM my father a peculiar form of indolence—not outright laziness so much as a gift for avoiding unpleasant chores without attracting public notice. My father took it almost as a matter of principle that most problems, if ignored, simply went away. And that his children were, more or less, among those problems. "I didn't even *talk* to you until you went away to college," he once said to me, as he watched me attempt to dress a six-month-old. "Your mother did all the dirty work."

This wasn't entirely true, but it'd pass cleanly through

any polygraph. For the tedious and messy bits of my childhood my father was, like most fathers of his generation, absent. (News of my birth he received by telegram.) In theory, his tendency to appear only when we didn't really need him should have left a lingering emotional distance; he should have paid some terrible psychological price for his refusal to suffer. But the stone cold fact is his children still love him, just as much as they love their mother. They don't hold it against him that he never addressed their diaper rash, or fixed their lunches, or rehearsed the lyrics to "I'm a Jolly Old Snowman." They don't even remember! My mother did all the dirty work, and without receiving an ounce of extra emotional credit for it. Small children are ungrateful; to do one a favor is, from a business point of view, about as shrewd as making a subprime mortgage loan.

When I became a father I really had only one role model: my own father. He bequeathed to me an attitude to the job. But the job had changed. I was equipped to observe, with detached amusement and good cheer, my children being raised. But a capacity for detached amusement was no longer a job qualification. The glory days were over.

This book is a snapshot of what I assume will one day be looked back upon as a kind of Dark Age of Fatherhood. Obviously, we're in the midst of some long unhappy transition between the model of fatherhood as practiced by my father and some ideal model, approved by all, to be practiced with ease by the perfect fathers of the future. But for now there's an unsettling absence of universal, or even local, standards of behavior. Within a few miles of my house I can find perfectly sane men and women who regard me as a Neanderthal who should do more to help my poor wife with the kids, and just shut up about it. But I can also find other perfectly sane men and women who view me as a Truly Modern Man and marvel aloud at my ability to be both breadwinner and domestic dervish—doer of an approximately 31.5 percent of all parenting. The absence of standards is the social equivalent of the absence of an acknowledged fair price for a good in a marketplace. At best, it leads to haggling; at worst, to market failure.

A brief thought experiment: Two couples—Bob and Carol, Ted and Alice—get together for dinner. They haven't known each other for long, and will discover during this dinner that they have cut slightly different parenting deals with their spouse. Carol and Bob split their parenting duties 60/40; Alice and Ted's split is more like 80/20. Bob and Carol think children shouldn't watch the Disney Channel; Ted and Alice think the Disney Channel, properly used, can be an excellent babysitter. After an otherwise delightful dinner they:

a. Go home and leave unmentioned how differently the other couple parents and divides the parenting chores.

b. Acknowledge their differences but agree, privately, to disagree. Parenting chores aren't chores at all: they're a joy! Plus, there's more than one way to skin a cat, or raise children.

c. Go home and haggle. Not right away, of course. Alice gets home and stews and promises herself she won't say anything. But at some point she fails to suppress the soundtrack in her head. "I really like the idea of reducing the influence Disney has on our family," she says. Or: "It's nice the way Bob drives the kids to school and frees up Carol in the mornings." Meanwhile, down the block, Bob is wondering why the hell he has to drive the kids to school *every* morning. Just before they agree that they won't be having sex anytime soon, he says, "Alice really is a great mom, isn't she?" And a funny thing happens: These two couples never see each other again. They had agreed to get together for dinner but somehow it never happens. Ted's busy; Carol can't make it.

If you answered (a) or (b) you can skip the next two paragraphs.

Here's the question: Why should social interaction with couples who parent even slightly differently so quickly lead to internal strife? How can putatively important and deeply considered decisions—how to parent, and what role the father should play—be so easily undermined by casual contact with a different approach? Why should even fictional representations of different parenting styles be an invitation to argue about who should do what?

One answer: In these putatively private matters people constantly reference public standards. They can live with their own parenting mistakes so long as everyone else is making the same ones. They don't care if they're getting a raw deal so long as everyone is getting the same deal. But there are no standards and it's possible there never again will be. We're all just groping, then lying about it afterward. As a result, the primary relationships in American family life have acquired the flavor of a Moroccan souk.

I began keeping a journal of my experience of fatherhood seven months after the birth of our first child. The reader will quickly see that I didn't set out to write about new fatherhood. I set out to write about Paris, but Paris was overshadowed by a seven-month-old baby. Most of what follows was written in the hazy, sleepless, and generally unpleasant first year after the birth of each of my three children. Most of it was also written within a few days after the incident reported. I found pretty quickly that any thoughts or feelings or even dramatic episodes I didn't get down on paper immediately I forgot entirely—which was the first reason I began to write stuff down. Memory loss is the key to human reproduction. If you remembered what new parenthood was actually like you wouldn't go around lying to people about how wonderful it is, and you certainly wouldn't ever do it twice.

Which brings me to the main reason I kept writing things down: this persistent and disturbing gap between what I was meant to feel and what I actually felt. Expected to feel overcome with joy—"It's a boy! You must be so happy!"—I often felt puzzled. (I shouldn't be just as happy if it was a girl?) Expected to feel outraged, I often felt secretly pleased; expected to feel worried, I often felt indifferent. ("It's just a little blood.") For a while I went around feeling a tiny bit guilty all the time, but then I realized that all around me fathers were pretending to do one thing, and feel one way, when in fact they were doing and feeling all sorts of things, and then engaging afterward in what amounted to an extended cover-up. As this book is largely a collection of stories, I'll use one that didn't make it in to illustrate the point. Cut to the journal . . .

We're at a fancy hotel in Bermuda. Like fancy hotels

everywhere, the place is paying new attention to the whims of small children. The baby pool is vast—nearly as big as the pool for the grown-ups, to which it is connected by a slender canal. In the middle of the baby pool is a hot tub, just for little kids. My two daughters, now ages six and three, leap from the hot tub into the baby pool and back again. The pleasure they take in this could not be more innocent or pure.

Then, out of nowhere, come four older boys. Ten, maybe eleven years old. As anyone who has only girls knows, boys add nothing to any social situation but trouble. These four are set on proving the point. Seeing my little girls, they grab the pool noodles—intended to keep three-year-olds afloat—and wield them as weapons. They descend upon Quinn, my six-year-old, whacking the water on either side of her, until she is almost in tears. I'm hovering in the canal between baby pool and grown-up pool, wondering if I should intervene. Dixie beats me to it. She jumps out in front of her older sister and thrusts out her three-year-old chest.

"TEASING BOYS!" she hollers, so loudly that grown-ups around the pool peer over their Danielle Steel novels. Even the boys are taken aback. Dixie, now on stage, raises her voice a notch:

"YOU JUST SHUT UP YOU STUPID MOTHERFUCKING ASSHOLE!"

To the extent that all hell can break loose around a baby pool in a Bermuda resort, it does. A John Grisham novel is lowered; several of Danielle Steel's vanish into beach bags. I remain hovering in the shallows of the grown-up pool where it enters the baby pool, with my entire head above water. My first thought: *Oh . . . my . . . God!* My second thought: *No one knows I'm her father.* I sink lower, like a crocodile, so that just my eyes and forehead are above the waterline; but in my heart a new feeling rises: pride. Behind me a lady on a beach chair shouts, "Kevin! Kevin! Get over here!"

Kevin appears to be one of the noodle-wielding eleven-year-old boys. "But Moooooooommm!" he says.

"Kevin! *Now!*"

The little monster skulks over to his mother's side while his fellow Orcs await the higher judgment. I'm close enough to hear her ream him out. It's delicious. "Kevin, did you teach that little girl those words?" she asks.

"Mooomm! Nooooooo!"

"Then where did she learn them?"

As it happens, I know the answer to that one: carpool. Months ago! I was driving them home from school, my two girls, plus two other kids—a seven-year-old boy and a ten-year-old girl. They were crammed in the back seat of the Volkswagen Passat, jabbering away; I was alone in the front seat, not especially listening. But then the ten-year-old said, "Deena said a bad word today."

"Which one?" asked Quinn.

"The S-word," said the ten-year-old.

"Ooooooooo," they all said.

"What's the S-word?" I asked.

"We can't say it without getting in trouble," said the ten-year-old knowingly.

"You're safe here," I said.

She thought it over for a second, then said, "Stupid."

"Ah," I said, smiling.

"Wally said the D-word!" said Quinn.

"What's the D-word?" I asked.

"Dumb!" she shouted, and they all giggled at the sheer illicit pleasure of it. Then the seven-year-old boy chimed in. "I know a bad word, too! I know a bad word, too!" he said.

"What's the bad word?" I asked brightly. I didn't see why he should be left out.

"Shutupyoustupidmotherfuckingasshole!"

I swerved off the road, stopped the car, and hit the emergency lights. I began to deliver a lecture on the difference between bad words and seriously bad words, but the audience was fully consumed with laughter. Dixie, especially, wanted to know the secret of making Daddy stop the car.

"Shutupmotherstupid fuck," she said.

"Dixie!" I said.

"Daddy," said Quinn thoughtfully, "how come you say a bad word when we spill something and when you spill something you just say, 'Oops'?"

"Stupidfuck!" screamed Dixie, and they all laughed.

"DIXIE!"

She stopped. They all did. For the rest of the drive they whispered.

So here we are, months later, in this Bermuda pool, Dixie with her chest thrust out in defiance, me floating like a crocodile and feeling very much different than I should. I should be embarrassed and concerned. I should be sweeping her out of the pool and washing her mouth out with soap. I don't feel that way. Actually, I'm impressed. More than impressed: awed. It's just incredibly heroic, taking out after this rat pack of boys. Plus she's sticking up for her big sister, which isn't something you see every day. I don't want to get in her way. I just want to see what happens next.

Behind me Kevin has just finished being torn what appears to be a new asshole by his mother, and is relaunching himself into the baby pool with a real malice. He's as indignant as a serial killer who got put away on a speeding ticket: He's guilty of many things but not of teaching a three-year-old girl the art of cursing. Now he intends to get even. Gathering his fellow Orcs in the hot tub, he and his companions once again threaten Quinn. Dixie, once again, leaps into the fray.

"TEASING BOYS!" she shouts. Now she has the attention of an entire Bermuda resort.

"YOU WATCH OUT TEASING BOYS! BECAUSE I PEED IN THIS POOL TWO TIMES! ONCE IN THE HOT POOL AND ONCE IN THE COLD POOL!"

The teasing boys flee, grossed out and defeated. Various grown-ups say various things to each other, but no one seeks to remove Dixie from the baby pool. Dixie returns to playing with her sister—who appears far less grateful than she should be. And the crocodile drops below the waterline, swivels, and vanishes into the depths of the grown-up pool. But he makes a mental note to buy that little girl an ice-cream cone. Even if her mother disapproves.

PART 1

QUINN

WE LANDED AT Charles de Gaulle Airport a couple of days before Christmas. One dog, one infant, nine books on how to get along with the French, and eleven pieces of luggage, three of which had already gone missing. We drove for ninety minutes in heavy traffic, the baby howling, the wife attempting to hide her exposed nursing bosom from the driver, and the dog scratching her bottom across the floor of the minivan. At length we arrived at our new home on the Left Bank, which we'd never actually seen, except in photographs. It was a small cluster of room-sized houses in a tiny garden tucked away at the back of a courtyard of an old apartment building. We piled out of the car and rushed to the front door, a small teeming peristaltic bundle of needs and hopes and anticipations. The door failed to open. The key mailed to us by the landlord did not fit the lock.

For the next thirty minutes, we sat in the cold, dark Paris courtyard and waited, mainly because we couldn't think what else to do. We were being punished for our sins; we had wanted to dance, now we were paying the fiddler. It had been fun, when people asked us where we lived, to say, "Well, that's hard to say, since at the end of the year we're moving to Paris." They were all envious, or pretended to be, which was just as gratifying. For the past six months we had been playing our new role: *People Who Are About to Live in Paris*. Now here we were, in Paris itself. We knew no one. We spoke so little French that it was better to claim we spoke none. We had no purpose. And that, I should have reminded myself, was the point.

About eighteen months earlier, my wife, Tabitha, and I were on an airplane when I began to complain about adulthood. One of the many things I dislike about being a grown-up is the compulsion to have a purpose in life. People are forever asking why you are doing whatever you happen to be doing and before long you succumb to the need to supply an answer. The least naturally ambitious people can have ambition thrust upon them in this way. Once you've established yourself as a more or less properly functioning adult, it is nearly impossible to just go somewhere and screw off.

Five months pregnant with our first child, Tabitha pointed out that the feeling of being weighed down by adulthood wasn't likely to improve anytime soon. Parenthood loomed. There was a time when I suspected this wouldn't have much effect on me. I figured that the chemical rush that attended new motherhood might get me off the hook—that Tabitha would happily embrace all the new unpleasant chores and I'd stop in from time to time to offer advice. She'd do the play-by-play; I'd do the color commentary. Five months into the pregnancy that illusion had been pretty well shattered by the anecdotal evidence. One friend with a truly amazing gift for getting out of things he did not want to do wrote to describe his own experience of fatherhood. "Remember that life you thought you had?" he wrote. "Guess what. It's not yours anymore."

At any rate, since a door in our lives seemed to be closing, we went looking for a window. As we sat on the plane, one thing led to another, and before long we had spread out on our laps the map of the world at the back of the in-flight magazine. We had no idea where we would wind up; we just knew we were going someplace foreign. My vague desire to live in Africa got swapped, unfairly I felt, for my wife's even vaguer one to live in Asia. Whole continents vanished from our future in an instant. After forty minutes we had shrunk the world to two cities: Barcelona and Paris. A few days later we were at a dinner party. The man across the table, an old friend, mentioned that his sister had this old, charming place in Paris occupied by tenants she couldn't stand. There it was: Our bluff was being called. We agreed to rent the place, sight unseen.

Now we are in Paris, in the cold and the dark, homeless and friendless and tongue-tied. Unbelievably, I hear myself asking: Why on earth did we come? Just then an elderly woman hobbles into the cobblestone courtyard and makes for the door nearest ours. Our new *French* neighbor! A distant memory lifts my spirits.

When I arrived in London to live outside the United States for the first time in my life, I was fitting the key into my new front door when an elderly woman called to me from the neighboring garden. "My name is Amanda Martin," she said in an ancient voice, "and I'll be your friend if you'll have me." Just like that, Amanda Martin had taken me into her life; I had a friend. She'd turned one hundred that year. The queen had sent her a telegram to congratulate her. When you know someone with that kind of standing in society, you somehow feel you belong, too. "Assimilation" is just another word for acquiring a bit of the local status.

I eye our new old French neighbor with longing. And even though I know that the moment history looks as if it is repeating itself is exactly the moment it is not, I feel a little leap in my spirits. I walk over, open a door for her, and say *bonjour*. She doesn't even look up, just keeps tap-tapping on by with her head down and right into her apartment. As she closes her door, the odor of stove gas wafts into the courtyard. A voice behind me says, "She's so old she forgets to turn off her gas burners when she goes out." I turn around. There stands a young man wearing a black stocking cap, a navy pea coat, and a grim expression. He looks like something dreamed up by Dostoyevsky, yet he sounds perfectly American. He motions to the door closing behind the elderly Frenchwoman: "One day she'll come back here, light a match, and this whole building will be a crater."

He puts his hand in the pocket of his pea coat. "I have your key," he says.

HERE IS HOW we spend the first half hour of every day in Paris:

Each morning between seven and seven-thirty, Quinn begins to sing. She's only eight months old, so she doesn't know any words. Still, she sounds as if she is practicing her scales. I crawl out of bed and tumble downstairs to turn on the heat, rigged by the French handyman so that it cannot run for more than about twelve hours on end without busting. I then clean up the mess invariably left by Vegas on the kitchen floor—one of several evil new tricks she has picked up from the local dogs—and toss her out into the garden. For a minute or so I watch through the window to make sure she doesn't get any ideas about the Camembert. Like French people, we now keep our smelly cheeses in planting pots outside. Imprisoned in the refrigerator, the Camembert still had the power to stink up the entire house. I'd open the door to grab a cold drink and be driven backward by the odor; a minute later, whoever was on the third floor would shout in panicky tones, "Shut the fridge! Shut the fridge!" Relations with the cheese had reached the point where one of us had to go.

Once Vegas is past the Camembert, I turn and race upstairs to snatch Quinn from her crib before she stops singing and becomes outraged. Coming up the stairs, I sing "Old MacDonald Had a Farm." On his farm he had a rooster, I assume. "Cock-a-doodle-doo" is the signal for Quinn to reach out with her arms and be lifted from her crib. Rising, she smiles and kicks her feet as if something really great is about to happen. I try not to disappoint. Together, we draw the curtains on the third-floor windows and peer up at the back of the crepuscular neighboring apartment building to see if any French people are doing anything particularly French. They are: sleeping. This is a nation of vampires; our streets are empty each morning until nearly ten. "Coo," Quinn says after a minute of staring at the old building, then swivels and tosses her warm little arms around me in her version of a bear hug.

As we move to the changing table the mood shifts. The moment she is laid on her back, Quinn loses her love for me and becomes as impatient as a race-car driver waiting for the tires to be changed. To keep her still enough to be unwrapped, cleaned, and then wrapped again, I must find ever more exotic ways to trick her into thinking something worth paying attention to is about to happen, right here, in her own bedroom. She never falls for the same trick twice. This morning, for instance, I danced the Parisian Trash Bag Dance—a performance she watched less with amusement than with a kind of morbid fascination. The Parisian Trash Bag Dance involves grabbing one of the giant blue trash bags they sell at the local market and swishing it back and forth over my head alluringly, while swaying my hips, like Salomé charming Herod. Once Quinn is mesmerized, I am able to remove one hand from the bag and do the dirty work, dancing all the while. A moment's pause in the entertainment and she's flipping herself onto her stomach, in a suicidal attempt to vault sideways off the changing table.

The diaper changed, I grab Quinn, put her under my arm like a football, duck beneath the low staircase ceiling, and plunge down the narrow, unbelievably steep stairs to our bedroom. There, Mother sleeps. There, for Quinn, is bliss. She raises her arms and cheers and kicks up such a delighted fuss that I am reminded all over again what a dull pleasure I am to my own child. I am the warm-up act. The featured attraction, inured to her own importance, reaches up from under her covers and drags Quinn under the covers.

Sadly, there is hardly a moment to spare on self-pity. By now there is the most unbelievable ruckus coming from outside. The dog, somehow already possessed of a

French dog's sense of her rights, is busy breaking down the door with her head. Sometimes, for fun, I open it just as she is about to strike again and she goes flying across the kitchen floor like a vaudeville comedian in a skit, crashing into the opposite wall.

LEAFING THROUGH A brochure that advertised "Activities for French Children," my wife came across an odd photograph. She held it up. It showed an infant and an adult swimming together underwater. It's hard to believe that a six-month-old baby could be taught to hold its breath and flap its arms and propel itself along the bottom of a swimming pool. But there it was, in black and white. The ad, so far as I could make out, went on to explain the importance of acclimating babies to water before they learned to be afraid of it. To that end, it offered thirty-minute private sessions in a womb-temperature pool. Bébé l'Eau, the company was called.

This struck me as a French twist on the business of preying on the insecurities of new parents. If you have a gift for frightening new parents, your fortune in this world is secure. New parents are not rational; they worry about all sorts of things that it makes no sense to worry about. For instance, I am at this moment worrying about when Quinn will learn to walk. I'd like to assume that our child will walk when she walks and that she'll do it well enough to get around. But my wife will not let me. She believes our child will walk only if we worry about it. Still, when was the last time you saw a full-grown adult crawling around the streets on all fours?

As I read the ad for Bébé l'Eau, it occurred to me that I never had any trouble learning how to swim. And I don't recall, as an infant, anyone ever treating me to any thirty-minute private sessions in womb-temperature water. But Tabitha's mind was already years ahead of mine. "What if she is afraid of water and never learns to swim?" she said. "What if she fell into a swimming pool?"

After a lot of phone calls, she finally got through to the authorities at Bébé l'Eau. We needed to fill out some forms, they said, which they'd send along. This sounded ominous. It was. A week later, a thick envelope arrived in our mailbox. Among other things, it contained one form that needed to be signed by a French pediatrician to prove that Quinn had been vaccinated, and another by a French GP to show that we adults had no rare skin diseases. Even back home this would seem like more trouble than it was worth.

But no: The life of our child was at stake. Tabitha became even more intent on gaining entry to Bébé l'Eau. If it required a great deal of effort, that was only because it was so desirable. She tried to persuade me that in addition to saving Quinn's life, it would also be fun. A *private* session in a giant pool brimming with womb-temperature water. She conjured up a vision of the three of us swimming happily together, underwater, released from the ordinariness of our daily lives.

It took two months of awkward phone calls in French and visits to the various doctors' offices, but she finally compiled the required paperwork and sent it to Bébé l'Eau. A few days later the authorities at Bébé l'Eau called. We were in. A private session.

On the appointed day, at the appointed hour (Sunday, crack of dawn), we climbed into a cab. Bébé l'Eau's neighborhood was curiously down-market; the address itself was merely a door leading to a long alley damp with mildew. We walked the length of it and emerged in an empty room lined with hard wooden benches. Paint flaked from the walls, an empty desk was stacked high with unopened mail. We sat on the bench and waited. Exclusive, perhaps, but in the wrong sense of the word.

After about ten minutes we heard, from a great distance, a splashing sound. It came from the end of yet another long corridor. We walked down it and found a closed door. It opened upon a scene. In a pool not much bigger than a large Jacuzzi frolicked a dozen scantily clad Frenchmen—two, I couldn't help but notice, with bright red rashes on their backs—and a half dozen children, several with snot running down their faces.

A Frenchman in a snorkel and mask and not much else floundered about, hollering instructions and waving plastic bathtub toys. Any sane person who wandered into the room would ask: Why are all these people crammed into this little tub?

I looked over at Tabitha. Tears pooled in her eyes. "They said it was private," she said.

"Who are you?" shouted the Frenchman in the snorkel. I explained, but it rang no bells.

"Come on in anyway!" he shouted.

There wasn't much else to do. And even though there hardly seemed room for three more bodies, we squeezed ourselves into the Jacuzzi. In doing so we entered the realm I have come to think of as Weird French Expertise. The French, of course, are famously expert on all sorts of rarefied subjects: wine, food, lovemaking, etc. But they are also expert in designating some slender body of learning as a "subject" and in establishing themselves as its sole authority. In the Luxembourg Gardens there is a woman who is a connoisseur of swings. Around the corner from our house is a club devoted to the scribblings of some obscure anthropologist. Our next-door neighbor holds meetings for those who are interested in Christopher Columbus's letters to his son.

It is no accident that Jacques Cousteau was French. The French know how to find categories ignored by the rest of the world and colonize them. Here, at Bébé l'Eau, was another example: baby dunking.

The point of what occurred during the next half hour remains a mystery to me. But there was, evidently, a point. The Frenchman in the mask and snorkel could not have been more earnest about his job. He ignored everyone else in the pool to focus on the newcomer. First he draped Quinn over a triangular flotation device. Then, just as the look of terror came into her eyes, he swooped her away and dragged her through the water on her back. Then, finally, as she began to howl, he dunked our only child's head under the surface of the womb-temperature water. Quinn came up spluttering and reaching desperately for her mother, who reached desperately back for her. But the Frenchman seemed highly pleased with the result. He asked if we would all come back next week, when we would make further progress.

But the strangest thing about this strange experience was how it ended. It is rare, even in a family of three, for everyone to be feeling the same emotion. But on the way out of Bébé l'Eau there was no question about it. We shared a moment. And the emotion we all felt was: satisfaction with a job well done.

ON THE RARE days I do my fair share of the parenting, the mood in Paris changes. This is true especially on the mornings I agree to escort Quinn to her twice-weekly Gymboree class. In the few minutes between the morning feeding and my racing out the door, baby in arms, in a long and often futile search for a taxicab, a single unspoken sentence echoes off our kitchen walls. The sentence is: "Now you will get a taste of what *my* life is like."

The truth is that parenting, in small doses, isn't as bad as all that. At the Gymboree office, I am once again treated as a charming oddity: the wonderful father who has taken the morning off from work to spend it with his baby daughter. About a third of the other adults are nannies; the rest are actual mothers. All of them find the notion of a man free in the middle of the day amusingly lovable, which is what, of course, I strive to be. From this and other evidence, I deduce that the French male has cut an even harsher deal with his spouse than the American one has. The American deal—or at any rate the American deal currently fashionable in my socioeconomic bracket—is that unless you can prove you are out making money, you had better at least pretend to be caring for your child. You might think that the French male, so conspicuous in his disdain for commerce, would be left holding the Gymboree bag more often. Alas, never, except on weekends, when he is unable to pretend that he is in his office.

A pleasant woman with a big smile has already plastered name tags onto the chests of the nine other babies in the class. All nine sit patiently on the floor, staring at each other's name tags like salesmen at a conference. Quinn wants no part of their act; when I put her down to sign us in, she hunches up into her peculiar crawling stance (straight-legged, knees off the ground, only palms of hands and bottoms of feet touching floor) and bolts for the room with the toys. By the time I catch up, she's halfway up a rubber staircase with a purple Wiffle ball in her mouth. She is deterred from her ascent only by the familiar Gymboree call to arms: *Bonjour, mes petits amis!*

The woman in charge of Gymboree has the manner of a Chief Mouseketeer, and even looks a bit like Annette Funicello. She prances into the room carrying a giant rag doll named Gymbo (pronounced JEEM-BO) and greets the babies in her falsetto singsong. (*"Bonjour, Quinn!"*) My great fear is that Quinn will do her usual worst, and swat either Gymbo or Ms. Gymbo upside the head, thus wrecking the Gymboree atmosphere, which is thick with at least the pretense of goodwill. But today, for whatever reason, she behaves and even seems to enjoy the rituals that open the Gymboree games. At the start of each class, each mother and pseudo-mother is required to grab her child beneath its armpits and drag it, behind Gymbo, in a goose-stepping parade around the gym. At the parade's conclusion, the parent is meant to squeal, "Wewewewewewewe," and hurl her baby into a pile with the other babies at the center of the room, at the feet of Ms. Gymbo.

Gymboree, I am told, is an American company. But it could not have found more fertile soil abroad in which to plant itself, importing, as it does, the love of order into a chaotic marketplace. Like Bébé l'Eau, it appears to be a carefully crafted, scientifically based institute for infant development. Just beneath the science, however, is an infant rendition of *Lord of the Flies*. Today, for example, Ms. Gymbo has strung from the various ladders, slides, tunnels, barrels, and seesaws that fill the room (and that the babies fight with each other to control) brightly colored sacks stuffed with pungent spices. In French too rapid for me to follow, she explains how important it is for infants to associate odors with places. I want to ask why; but after a minute or two she's lost me, and it takes all my mental energy to figure out what I'm supposed to do next with Quinn. What I'm supposed to do next, apparently, is to lead her by the nose around the room and persuade her to take big whiffs of the various sacks. But Quinn, who has yet to read Proust, has no interest in olfactory associations. Her eyes remain fixed on the purple Wiffle ball, which has rolled off, odorlessly, into a corner.

This creates the usual problem of disguising my child's lack of interest in personal development. If Ms. Gymbo notices that Quinn's father is neglecting his duties, she will come over and speak to me sweetly in her rapid falsetto French, to the vast amusement of the French mothers. Thus Quinn and I cut a deal: I allow her to race up ladders and down ramps after her purple Wiffle ball and ignore the spice bags until Ms. Gymbo turns her attention to us, whereupon I grab the nearest sack and thrust it against her nose, with the insistence of a bank robber chloroforming a security guard. However, Quinn reneges on the deal, shrieks, and cries real tears. "*Très bien!*" says Ms. Gymbo, and, to my relief, moves on. When she's gone I stick my own nose into the offending sack. It smells, distinctly and pungently, of dog shit. What kind of experiment is this? I want to ask but of course don't. Has Ms. Gymbo stuffed dog shit into one of the sacks as, perhaps, the control?

French Gymboree ends, as it began, with a slightly frightening group ritual. The babies are once again heaped together at the center of the room, where the bigger ones torture the smaller ones to tears. Then Ms. Gymbo blows bubbles over them. The babies all love this, and for a brief moment something like harmony reigns. But at precisely that moment, Ms. Gymbo puts away her bubbles and drags out her multicolored parachute. Anyone looking for evidence that babies have minds of their own need only observe one Gymboree parachute ritual. When they are piled up on the parachute and dragged around the room by us mothers as we sing some incomprehensible French song, they become, as one, solemn. And when their mothers help Ms. Gymbo make a tent of the parachute, and make to drop it onto their heads, all hell breaks loose. You've never seen a baby crawl until you have seen it trying to escape a Gymboree parachute descending upon its little head. Within seconds babies are here, there, and everywhere except where they are meant to be. The chute hits nothing but bare ground, and the class ends, as always, in chaos.

The twenty minutes in the taxi home are spent in tears and recuperation. But by the time we arrive, we are able to smile and preserve the conceit that a father likes nothing better than to spend a morning with his child.

AT SOME POINT in the last few decades, the American male sat down at the negotiating table with the American female and—let us be frank—got fleeced. The agreement he signed foisted all sorts of new paternal responsibilities on him and gave him nothing of what he might have expected in return. Not the greater love of his wife, who now was encouraged to view him as an unreliable employee. Not the special love from his child, who, no matter how many times he fed and changed and wiped and walked her, would always prefer her mother in a pinch. Not even the admiration of the body politic, who pushed him into signing the deal. Women may smile at a man pushing a baby stroller, but it is with the gentle condescension of a high officer of an army toward a village that surrendered without a fight. Men just look away in shame. And so the American father now finds himself in roughly the same position as Gorbachev after the fall of the Berlin Wall. Having shocked the world by doing the decent thing and ceding power without bloodshed for the sake of principle, he is viewed mainly with disdain. The world looks at him schlepping and fetching and sagging and moan-

ing beneath his new burdens and thinks: OH . . . YOU . . .
POOR . . . BASTARD.

But I digress.

I came home one night, relieved the babysitter, and
found that Quinn had three bright red spots on her
forehead and, for the first time in her life, a fever. The
domestic policy handbook clearly states that when anything goes seriously wrong with our child, I am to holler for her mother and then take my place at her elbow
and await further instructions. As I say, the American
father of a baby is really just a second-string mother.
But the first string was nowhere to be found. For the
first time our child badly needed help that, it appeared,
only I could provide. On the heels of that realization
followed another: After a year of watching Quinn claw
toward her mother whenever she became upset, I now
could prove my own qualifications for the job.

A single phone call to a miraculous service called
SOS Médicins fetched up a nattily clad French doctor to
our doorstep inside five minutes. He arrived in a little
white truck with a cross on the side that looked a bit
like an old World War I ambulance. He was easily the
most reassuring doctor I have ever met; there was not a
hint of self-doubt about the man. Treating a sick baby
is more like treating a sick dog than a sick person, as the

baby can't tell you where it hurts. To our new French doctor this proved no obstacle at all. He marched into the house, spotted Quinn giggling on the couch, smiled knowingly, and said, "*Varicelle*."

Chicken pox. Having diagnosed the disease from a distance of fifteen feet, he then examined the howling patient for another three minutes. On top of the chicken pox, he found ear and throat infections, plus the fever I already knew about, plus a couple of unrelated, smaller defects. He was so efficient at finding diseases that I thought he would find she had the plague or something, but his work was so quick and self-assured that it was impossible to question any of it. Afterward, he sat down at our kitchen table and wrote out two long pages of prescriptions, all of them illegible, and said that he was certain she'd feel better once she'd taken a few of them. From start to finish, his visit took about fifteen minutes and cost less than forty bucks. *Vive la France!*

I trundled the prescriptions together with Quinn across the street to the pharmacy—everything in Paris you might want to buy always seems to be just across the street—and came away with a huge plastic sack of cures. Then, with a truly fantastic display of heretofore unrevealed parental competence, I actually persuaded my child to swallow several of them.

All this was perfectly thrilling, and not simply because

there is an obvious pleasure in curing one's child. Power was in the air. It was a rare fatherhood Al Haig moment: I was in charge here.

Then Tabitha walked into the house.

"What's going on?"

I told her everything that had happened, and as I did, tears welled in her eyes. Mistaking their meaning, I could not have been more pleased with myself. I assumed she was *moved* by my performance. At this difficult moment in our child's life, when she would naturally look to her mother for comfort, her mother was away and unreachable. Plucked from the end of the bench and sent into the game with just seconds on the clock, I'd been told to take the final shot. I'd hit nothing but net.

I waited for what I was certain would be a curtain call. Instead, there was only silence. I could see from her face that she wasn't merely upset; she was irritated. She walked over to the sink and banged around some dirty dishes. With whom was she irritated? I wondered, neglecting the important truth, corollary to the rule about the fool at the poker table, that if you don't know who your wife is pissed off at, it's you.

"Why are you so upset?" I asked. "The worst is over— it's all taken care of."

"I just wish I had been . . . here."

"But why?"

"If I was here I could have asked the questions."

All of a sudden, my questions weren't good enough. How would she know? She banged the dishes around a bit more, and then said, "Did you ask the doctor *why* he was sure all these medicines were the right ones?"

"Uh, no." Of course I hadn't. He was the doctor.

"Did you ask him why, if it is chicken pox, she's had these red spots before?"

"She has?"

"Did you ask why they are only on her face?"

Upon review of the videotape, my three-point shot was nullified, the team went down in defeat, and I was sent back to the end of the bench. I was unable to answer even one of the questions that a genuinely caring parent would have thought to ask. "The doctor said that the spots would spread to the rest of her body by tomorrow," I said, answering one that hadn't been asked.

"I think we ought to call another doctor," she said, then swept her child up in her arms and took her away to whatever place mothers take their children when they don't want their husbands to follow. Once they'd left, I quickly, and for the first time, read the instructions on the medicine. The first two bottles I selected said, chillingly, "NOT FOR CHILDREN UNDER 6 YEARS OF AGE." The bottle I believed to contain a chicken pox ointment proved, on close inspection, to be a sore-throat spray. The gunk I'd been told to apply to the pox itself was not a spray, as the forty-dollar home-delivery French doctor had told me it would be, but a strangely dry powder that was impossible to apply to anything, unless you happened to have Krazy Glue. Left alone with her father, our child stood no chance of survival.

The next day came, and the red spots refused to spread, and the fever subsided. The day after that, the fever had gone altogether, and the spots had faded to nothing. To me this was a very good sign: Quinn was cured. No, I had cured Quinn. The doctor had said that there were rare light cases of chicken pox in which the spots didn't spread: Here was one. To my wife it was a sign that the doctor had queered the diagnosis and that our child must be ailing from some other, heretofore undiagnosed disease. "I want to take her to the hospital," she said.

The language of parenthood is encoded. When a mother says to a father, "I want to take her to the hospital," she is really saying "WE are ALL going to the hospital, and if you whisper even a word of complaint, you will have proved yourself for all time a man incapable of love." Maternal concern is one of those forces of nature not worth fighting.

Off we went to find a taxi, and then to find a hospital.

Once we did so, we were seated in a small waiting room jammed with toys in which Quinn showed little interest, clinging, as she was, to her mother. Twenty minutes later, we were greeted by another nattily clad doctor, who was, if anything, even more self-assured than the first. He took one look at Quinn, laughed loudly, and said, "Not chicken pox."

Tabitha looked pleased. "Then what are these?" I asked, pointing to the faded spots on Quinn's forehead.

"Insect bites," he said.

I handed him the spray and asked why the doctor had instructed me to apply it to chicken pox.

"I don't know. This is sore-throat spray. Who told you your daughter had chicken pox?"

I gave him the whole story and handed him the two pages of prescriptions, which, as it happened, had the name of the doctor who had written them on top. This provoked only more laughter. "Dr. D___," he said, "he doesn't know anything about children's medicine."

"You *know* him?"

"He's my golfing partner." He was still laughing; this was the best joke he'd heard all day.

"Is he a good golfer?"

"Very! He spends very little time working as a doctor."

On the way home in the car, the family spirits could

not have been higher. Quinn was cured—or as good as cured—and well, nestling up against her mother. I was back on the end of the bench. And there, with my incompetence in dealing with matters critical to my child's survival fully exposed, I was once again well loved. Some sort of natural order had been restored.

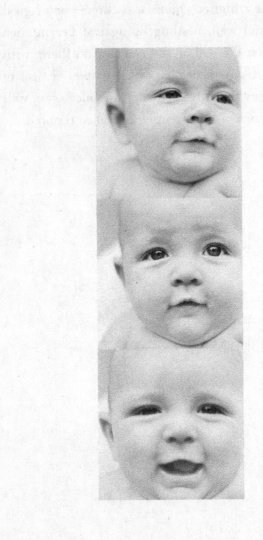

PART 2

DIXIE

MY MAIN AMBITION when my wife went into labor was to be sober. When our first child was born, I'd been rushing to finish a book. I'd suspected, rightly, that it would be impossible to reconcile book production with new fatherhood. To finish the manuscript before the baby arrived I'd taken to drinking several cups of coffee after dinner and working right through the night. I'd quit around four in the morning, then knock myself out with cheap wine. When Tabitha's water broke I'd just thrown back a third glass of unsentimental Chardonnay. I'd wound up driving her to the hospital at five miles per hour and then, somewhat dramatically, passing out on her delivery room bed. I'd woken up just in time to witness the birth of my first child (Quinn Tallulah Lewis) but had made, I fear, a poor impression. For the past two years and eleven months I have been on the wrong end of a story called "How My Husband Was Loaded When My Baby Was Born." I promised myself I'd do better this time. It was my last chance.

I remember that it was a Monday evening, just before cocktail hour, when Tabitha said she felt funny. An hour later we were in triage; an hour after that we were walking up and down the hospital halls to accelerate her labor to the point where it generated the respect of the women who doled out delivery rooms. I knew this hospital, from hazy experience. I recalled dimly the secret kitchen stocked with grape juice and the crushed ice and the strawberry Popsicles. I remembered vaguely how to finagle a private recovery room. I was the college graduate who had partied his way through school and was now returning on alumni day, hoping his classmates had forgotten what he'd been like. The one thing I knew for sure was that when they asked you if you wanted to get back in your car and endure labor in the intimacy of your own home, or take the hospital room now, you took the hospital room now. Having done this, I settled into the chair beside Tabitha's bed and watched nurses string nine separate tubes and wires from her body to various machines: narcotics drip, penicillin drip, thermometers, blood pressure gauges, gas masks to deliver pure oxygen, heart monitors for baby and mother, and God knows what else.

And then . . . nothing. For the next ten hours we sat around with expectant looks, like extras in a World War II movie battle scene waiting for the Japanese finally to come charging through the jungle. From the point of view of the woman, "labor" is well named; from the point of view of the man, it really should be called "waiting." Your wife goes into labor; you go into waiting.

A woman in labor needs to believe, however much evidence she has to the contrary, that the man in waiting beside her bed is directing every ounce of his concern toward her. This is of course impossible; and so the trick for the man in waiting is to disguise his private interests. He learns to camouflage trips to the john as grape-juice-fetching missions. When he is hungry he waits until his wife dozes off, then nips furtively down to the hospital vending machine for his supper of Ring Dings and Nacho Cheese Doritos. At some point in his private ordeal one of the hospital staff will turn to him and ask sweetly, "And how is Dad doing?" He must understand that no one actually cares how Dad is doing. His fatigue, his worries, his tedium, his disappointment at the contents of hospital vending machines—these are better unmentioned. Above all, he must know that if his mask of perfect selflessness slips for even a moment he will be nabbed.

"Would a little food taste good to you right now?"

"I don't think so." (Muffled, through oxygen mask.)

"Because they have these Ring Dings in the vending machine. The kind with the vanilla icing."

The fixed accusing stare. "You're incredible." Pause. A weary tone. "If you want something to eat, just go get something to eat."

At great and tedious length, fourteen hours after labor began, the baby made its dash for the exit. Then it stopped. The doctor on call poked and prodded a bit, then took off her gloves and stared.

Then another doctor appeared, Tabitha's doctor, conveniently just back from vacation. Tabitha's doctor is maybe the least likely obstetrician in Berkeley, California. He doesn't believe, for example, in the sanctity of his patients' whims. He has no time for superstition; he is unapologetic about his belief in the power of modern science; he believes that the best way to endure childbirth is not out in the woods surrounded by hooting midwives but in a hospital bed, numb from the waist down. He is, in short, my kind of guy. Maybe my favorite thing about him is the way he dismisses ignorant fears with such contempt that they simply vanish. When he is around, Tabitha feels, rightly, that she is in more capable hands than her own. This, for her, counts as an unusual experience.

Tabitha's doctor collected information from the doctor on call, in the way doctors do. They spoke for maybe two minutes, in English as intelligible as their handwriting. At some point I remembered that it was my job to know what was going on.

"What's up?" I asked.

"The baby wants to come out face first," said the doctor on call.

"And that's not good?"

"It won't fit," said Tabitha's doctor. He let that unpleasant thought hang in the air.

"We can't get a grip on it to turn it around," said the doctor on call.

Without ever uttering the phrase "C-section," the two doctors conveyed the idea of it well enough. As Tabitha's doctor leaned in to see what he could do, I leaned over Tabitha and, drawing upon my years of selling bonds for Salomon Brothers, tried to persuade her of all the advantages to having her stomach cut open. She pretended to nod and agree, but tears welled in her eyes. The doctors, to their credit, noticed her distress; and, to their even greater credit, they responded to it. Before I knew how it happened, Tabitha's doctor brandished a large pair of suction cups, one over each hand.

"I'm going to try to pull this baby out," he said, in a different tone. He was no longer a doctor. He was a deep sea fisherman. One of those guys who sat on the back of big motorboats hauling in schools of giant tuna with one hand while drinking beer with the other.

Tabitha's head popped off the pillow. "If it puts the baby at any risk I'd rather have the C-section," she said.

"Tabitha, no shit." The doctor shook his head and pretended to say to me what he wanted to say to himself. "I love the way her mind works. Just what I want to do, put the baby at risk."

Ten minutes later, by some miracle I still do not understand, he was hauling a baby girl into the world. I knew from experience that the little involuntary sob of joy I made as my eyes met Tabitha's was a fleeting sensation. I also knew that other, less understandable emotions would soon follow.

THE LAST PLACE to recover from what they do to you in a hospital is a hospital. When Tabitha staggered down the hall from her delivery room to her recovery room, she left a place where people had cared for her so well that it brought tears to my eyes, and entered a place where she was a nuisance. You might think that people who work in hospital maternity wards have some special feeling for new mothers. You'd be wrong. Some of them enter the spirit of the occasion, and a few do it with obvious pleasure. But an astonishing number seem to resent any woman who has had the nerve to reproduce. To ensure that she thinks twice before she does it again, they bang bedpans against her door every twenty minutes, holler down the halls all hours of the night, ignore all her gentle requests, and, in general, exude the warmth and charm of an old Soviet border guard. "Oh, great, another fucking baby," I half expected a few of them to say as they breathed their heavy sighs over my wife's pale, spent body. For all I know, this is sound hospital strategy. Certainly, the atmosphere in the recovery ward discourages anyone from staying longer than necessary. The patient remains on the premises just long enough for the hospital to collect the data it needs to prove to the courts that it didn't kill her.

Anyway, the last time around there was no question about what I would do after our child was born: I'd curl up in a little ball in the chair beside my wife's hospital bed, protect her from the hospital staff, and pop down to the nursery every half hour or so to make sure that Quinn hadn't been sold on the black market. This time is different. This time I'm free to go; indeed, it is my duty to go. By default, I'm now in charge of family harmony. Which is to say, I'm supposed to fetch Quinn from home, bring her to the hospital, and prove to her that her life, as promised, is now better than ever.

The past few months Tabitha ginned up what we both imagined to be a ruthlessly effective propaganda campaign to brainwash our two-and-a-half-year-old into thinking that the arrival of Dixie, and the subsequent collapse in her share of parental attention, was actually in her interest. Out went Dr. Seuss and in came *I'm a Big Sister!* and *Hush, Don't Wake the Baby*. Each night, Quinn laid her head on her mother's swelling belly and engaged her imaginary sibling in loving conversation. A few weeks back, I even drove her over to the hospital, walked her through a play-by-play of the birth, and, to encourage her to think of this as a win-win situation, bought her a chocolate doughnut from the hospital vending machine.

When I got home from the hospital, I found Quinn as delighted as ever with life. "Daddy!" she cried as she freed herself from the babysitter and threw herself into my arms. Then it dawned on her something was missing. "Where's Mama?" she asked.

"Mama had the baby!" I said. "A baby girl! You're a big sister!"

"But where is Mama?" She was no longer a happy, loving child. She was a personal injury lawyer taking a deposition.

"In the hospital! With Dixie!"

"I want my family back," she said.

"But now you have even *more* family. We have Dixie, too."

"I hate Dixie," she said. Then she howled and bared her teeth.

It was an unpromising start. In this situation an unprepared father, a father who hadn't done his homework, might say something foolish. He might say, for instance, "That's not a nice thing to say," or "Of course you don't hate Dixie. You love Dixie. She's your sister." But I'd read the parenting texts, or at any rate the passages Tabitha highlighted and dropped in my inbox. I'd listened intently to the many reports Tabitha brought back from the parenting classes she attended every week. I'd taken note of the instructional parenting cartoon Tabitha glued to our refrigerator. I understood that my job was no longer to force the party line upon Quinn. My job was to *validate* her feelings.

"You hate Dixie because you're afraid she's taken Mama away," I said.

"Yes," she said.

"Yes," I repeated. And then . . . I was stumped. I couldn't think of what to say next. All I could think was: *Of course you hate Dixie. She* has *taken Mama away. I'd hate her, too, if I were you.* Truth is, a tiny part of me was proud that she saw the situation for what it was, a violation of her property rights. It boded well for her future in the free market.

The parenting books don't tell you where to go when your first move doesn't lead to psychological checkmate. The only thing I had going for me was the toddler's indifference to logic.

"So you want to go see Dixie?" I said.

"To the hospital?"

"To the hospital."

She thought about this. "Can I have a chocolate doughnut?" she asked.

The hospital visit went well enough. The doughnut purchased the hour needed to initiate the first of the peace talks. But that night, when I put Quinn to bed, something was not quite right. First, she insisted that I lay her head at the foot of her bed and her feet at the head. Then she demanded three books and two stories instead of her usual two and one. Finally, as I switched off her light, she said, "In fact, you forgot to give me a kiss." I gave her a kiss. "A kiss doesn't make all the angry go away," she said. And then: "Good night, Daddy," in a voice I'd never before heard. A chillingly adult-sounding voice.

An hour later there came from her room a sudden noise. She was still awake, fiddling furiously with something on her floor. It was a book of family photos, given to her by her grandmother, which had given her a year of pleasure. She'd yanked it to pieces and scattered them across the room.

IN WADING THROUGH the parenthood literature, I have read exactly one piece of writing that comes close to capturing the potential misery of it. It was an article in *The New Yorker* by John Seabrook, in which the author hunted down a man named Ferber, whose research gave birth to a cold-blooded method of training babies to sleep. As I recall, Seabrook and his wife had been made miserable by their newborn's tendency to holler through the night. Addled by lack of sleep, they set out to "Ferberize" their child. This meant shutting the door and clinging to each other as their baby in the next room shrieked with greater and greater urgency. Ferber extremists believe that parents should leave their infant to learn how to fall asleep on its own, even if the poor creature becomes so upset it vomits. One book even suggests that parents spread a plastic sheet under the baby's crib to catch the mess. Before Seabrook went this far, he set out to find Ferber. When he found him, he also found that Ferber had recanted. He was no longer quite so sure about his early research. Millions of babies were being tortured without a theory.

Even if we had a theory, we couldn't abide by it. It's unnatural to leave a baby to cry alone in its crib; it makes you feel about as humane as a serial killer. And so our lives have now resumed a pattern they last had three years ago, when Quinn was born. Only this time it's worse because Quinn is still here. Dixie—who is now referred to by the other three members of her family simply as "the baby"—wakes up every hour between seven p.m. and seven a.m. and bleats just loudly enough to alert Quinn to the possibilities. Quinn wakes up at eleven at night, then again at one, three, and five-thirty in the morning, and each time screams a horror-movie scream that sends a chill down the spine of the man across the street.

There is no way my wife and I could function if we each had to deal with both children, and so we've split the family in two. I sleep downstairs with Quinn, Tabitha sleeps upstairs with Dixie. On good nights, we meet for dinner. Essentially, we are both single parents. I reckon that Tabitha averages maybe three hours of sleep each night, broken up into forty-five-minute chunks. I get more like five broken hours, and while I should be pleased about that, I am, in truth, pissed off. That's what happens when you don't sleep properly for long stretches: You get pissed off. At any rate, that's what happens to me. My wife grows melancholy.

I decided to keep this diary for a couple of reasons. The first was that I wanted a written record for Dixie, who, as a second child, runs a risk of being a blur; and I knew that there was no way I would take the trouble to record her arrival if I didn't have an editor breathing down my neck for the material. The other was that I noticed a tendency to gloss over the unpleasant aspects of parenthood, in part because it's unseemly to complain about one's children but also because there is a natural inclination to forget that there was anything to complain about. But there is. In the first few weeks after a child is born—or at least after a child of mine is born—it is as if someone must pay for whatever it endured when it exited the womb and entered the world.

Here's what my typical day now looks like, for example, beginning at what used to be bedtime. I awaken at eleven at night, and then again at one, three, and five-thirty in the morning, to persuade Quinn that there isn't a spider in her bed. At seven a.m. she rises for good, somehow fully rested, and hollers at the top of her lungs for her mother. As battered as Rocky going into the twelfth round against Apollo Creed, I wrestle her to the ground, dress her in clothes she does not want to wear, and drag her out of the house, still screaming, to my office, where I feed her a breakfast she does not want to eat. She demands chocolate; I offer a fruit plate; after tantrums on both sides of the bargaining table, we compromise on an Eggo waffle. Around nine

I get her to school and enjoy a brief feeling of self-satisfaction: I am coping manfully with a great big mess. I'm preventing my wife from further suffering. I am the good soldier who has leapt on the hand grenade, so that others may live.

This cheering thought lasts until I get home and find my wife in tears. Often I try to hide, but usually she spots me, and when she does, she will usually say something poignant. "I feel like I am going through this alone," for instance. Or, "I don't know how much more of this I can take." Whatever she says neatly undercuts my belief that I am carrying far more than my share of our burden; indeed, it makes it clear that I am not a hero at all but a slacker, a deadbeat Dad. Demoralized, I tromp back down to my office and try for a few hours without success to put bread on the table, before retrieving Quinn from school.

By about the sixth day of this routine, I am as random as a misfiring piston and as raw as an exposed nerve. Driving Quinn home the other day, for instance, I was cut off by a woman in a station wagon. "What the fuck are you doing, lady?" I shouted at the windshield hysterically.

"Daddy, why did you say fuckyoudoing?" a voice inquired from the back seat.

"Oh." Pause. "That's not what I said."

"Was she a fucky lady?"

"*Funky*. Funky lady."

"You said fucky."

Once home, there is paid help—for which I feel *guilty*, if you can believe that—and I try to use it to get back to work. In truth, I usually wind up curled up in a little ball of fatigue until dinner, which is my job to throw together. After dinner, I put Quinn to bed while Tabitha nurses the baby for the twenty-thousandth time. Then the cycle begins all over again.

I know that all of this will soon pass and our family will once more achieve some wonderful new equilibrium. With one more person on hand to love and to be loved, we'll soon be drowning in finer feelings. But for now we're drowning mainly in self-pity.

You would think that someone would have come up with a humane, economical method for absorbing a new child into a family. Certainly there's billions in it for whoever does. As it stands, there are three approaches to the problem, all of them inadequate. You can pretend to believe the books and do whatever you must do to your children to ensure a good night's sleep for yourself. You can throw money at it and hire squadrons of night nurses to tend to your children while you move into the local Ritz-Carlton. Or you can do what we are doing and muddle through as best as you can, grabbing at any old piece of advice that comes your way, less because it will actually help matters than because it offers hope. You tell yourself that eventually this baby will learn to sleep, just as eventually it will learn to walk and to use the toilet. After all, you don't see a lot of adults who wake up hollering at the ceiling every forty-five minutes, just as you don't see a lot of adults who crawl around on all fours, or who crap their pants twice a day. So it stands to reason that the problem will solve itself. Here's hoping.

THE OTHER DAY on the way to school Quinn demanded, unusually, that I shut off the nursery rhymes. Then, even more unusually, she sat silently, staring straight ahead, ignoring my attempts to engage her in conversation. I tilted the rearview mirror to make sure she wasn't choking on something and was greeted with a gaze of what I can only describe as mad intensity. Finally she said, "My Daddy is dead."

Four weeks ago, before the birth of Dixie, this would have shocked me. Now it's almost pleasantly familiar. Quinn's going through a dark phase. A week ago she came home from school with a stack of drawings. Gone were the blue and pink pastels she had favored since she'd first become a prolific artist. In their place were many disturbing furious black scrawls. One horrifying ink and crayon sketch resembled an ax-murdered spider. My child had entered her first new period.

"Oh, so now I'm dead?" I said cheerily.

"You stink, Daddy," she said.

"Am I dead or do I stink?"

She thought it over. "Both."

On some days she hollers insults at me the whole way to school—"You stink" and "You're dead" are two favorites—and if she can find something to hurl at my head, she'll do that, too. Driving her around these days is like playing right field for the visiting team in Yankee Stadium.

The division of responsibility that's followed the birth of a second child has left me exposed in whole new ways. With Tabitha essentially glued to Dixie, I am the only outlet for Quinn's understandable need to scream at her parents. I am also her main parental influence. I confess I hadn't realized the implications of this until the other night when, after a brutalizing day in which I foolishly agreed to take both children myself so that their mother might go to San Francisco, I was tiptoeing out of the room containing mother and nursing child and aiming myself in the general direction of the sofa bed. Mother seemed glum. "What's the matter?" I asked, not particularly caring for the answer. Out gushed a torrent of complaints about Quinn's behavior since Dixie's birth. She'd become surly with babysitters; she'd stopped sleeping through the night; she no longer ate her vegetables; she was resisting the final, crucial stages of potty training; she showed no interest in any activity except watching *Shrek* for the 150th time; she'd been rude to her mother when she returned from San Francisco.

In the good old days when Tabitha complained to me

about Quinn, she did so in a collaborative spirit. We were joined by common interests; we were Munger and Buffett hashing out investment strategy. This didn't sound like that. This sounded more like an Arab attempting to engage an American on the subject of the Israeli army.

"She's not eating her vegetables because she's pissed off about Dixie," I said.

"She's not eating her vegetables because she had a huge cup of Frosted Mini-Wheats just before dinner," she said.

The Frosted Mini-Wheats had been my idea. She didn't say that; she didn't have to. Everything about Quinn was now my idea. My wife knew this was the time in Quinn's life when she needed to be indulged. But she also had an investment to protect.

"I just feel like my two and a half years of work on her is being washed down the drain," she said.

"She'll get all her good habits back once she gets used to Dixie."

"Once you lose good habits you can't get them back," she said.

Never having had good habits myself, I was poorly situated to argue the point, and if I had, I wouldn't have been believed. My wife was raised in a military household that left her in full possession of the martial virtues. I was raised in a home where it was possible for me every couple of weeks to steal a jumbo sack of Nestlé's chocolate-chip cookies from the kitchen and secrete them under my bed at night without anyone being the wiser for it. I was meant to be six-foot-three and make straight A's through high school but as a result of skipping dinner and instead eating a dozen Nestlé's chocolate-chip cookies every night I wound up five-foot-ten with a D in biology my sophomore year. I could see my wife's point. She had spent two and a half years drilling her better qualities into her first child only to see them sucked out in three and a half weeks of prolonged exposure to me. She was the ace of the pitching staff who had shut down the opposing batters for eight innings only to watch the closer blow the game in the ninth. (I've had baseball on my mind.)

In the past three years I have tried on occasion to imagine what effects I am having on my child. I do this dutifully rather than naturally because it seems like the sort of thing a father should do. But I never get anywhere with it. The fact, as opposed to the theory, of life with a small child is an amoral system of bribes and blackmails. You do this for me, you get that. You don't do this for me, you don't get that. I've always assumed that if a small child has enough joy and love and stability in her life, along with intelligently directed bribes and blackmail, the rest will take care of itself. And my approach appeared to be working. Right up until the birth of her sister, Quinn excelled at childhood and did so, it seemed, effortlessly. It honestly never occurred to me that I should be in some way *shaping* her. I was one of those easygoing CEOs who believe that excessive discipline crushes the creativity of his employees. I believed in managing by hanging around.

In retrospect, the only reason I was able to get away with this pose is that I wasn't the CEO. I was more like a titular chairman, allowed to sit at the head of the table but never actually listened to. Now, clearly, I must take a different approach. The CEO's attention has been diverted by a difficult acquisition in a foreign country. The chairman is, however briefly, in charge. Everyone else is anxious.

THE THING THAT most surprised me about fatherhood the first time around was how long it took before I felt about my child what I was expected to feel. Clutching Quinn after she exited the womb, I was able to generate tenderness and a bit of theoretical affection, but after that, for a good six weeks, the best I could manage was detached amusement. The worst was hatred. I distinctly remember standing on a balcony with Quinn squawking in my arms and wondering what I would do if it wasn't against the law to hurl her off it. I also recall convincing myself that official statistics dramatically overstated the incidence of sudden infant death syndrome—when an infant dies for no apparent reason in her crib—because most of them were probably murder. The reason we all must be so appalled by parents who murder their infants is that it is so easy and even natural to do. Maternal love may be instinctive, but paternal love is learned behavior.

Here is the central mystery of fatherhood, or at any rate my experience of it. How does a man's resentment of this . . . *thing* . . . that lands in his life and instantly disrupts every aspect of it for the apparent worse turn into love? A month after Quinn was born, I would have felt only an obligatory sadness if she had been rolled over by a truck. Six months or so later, I'd have thrown myself in front of the truck to save her from harm. What happened? What transformed me from a monster into a father? I do not know. But this time around I'm keeping a closer eye on the process.

I can't honestly say that I've found Dixie, at least at first glance, quite so loathsome as her older sister. She doesn't holler so much for no reason at all, and when she does, I'm usually not around to hear it, as I'm taking care of Quinn. That's the main difference this time: I now have what her mother regards as a good excuse to avoid the unpleasantness of these first few weeks, and so I do. Occasionally I even forget that she's there. It's a strange sensation to walk into a room, flip on the television, watch a baseball game for twenty minutes, look to your right, and find a five-week-old child you did not know was there looking back. Still, I've been left knowingly alone with Dixie enough, and been made sufficiently unhappy by her with fatigue and frustration, to have felt the odd Murderous Impulse. At the same time, I have already noticed, in the past week or so, a tendency to gaze upon her with genuine fondness. Here as best I can determine are the factors contributing to what appears to be another miraculous shift in feeling occurring inside me at this very moment:

1. Maternal propaganda. I am a professional writer and therefore am meant to be keenly observant. Without Tabitha, however, I would notice next to nothing about my own child, and certainly nothing admirable. All I am able to see by myself are the many odd-colored substances that emerge from her that need cleaning up, and the many unpleasant noises she makes that shake me from my sleep. But there are all these other, more lovable things about her, too, and her mother sees every one of them and presses them upon me with such genuine enthusiasm that it thaws my frozen heart. Her facial expressions, for instance. She has her Smurf Face and her Bowel-Movement Face and her E.T. Face. She has her How-Ya-Doin'-Today Face and her Call-Me-at-the-Office Face and her Mafia-Hit-Man Face—which is the one when she curls her lip at you and you half expect her to say, "You talkin' to me?"

2. Her gift for mimicry. A five-week-old baby is for the most part unresponsive to ordinary attempts to communicate with her. You can scream at her or you can sing to her, and all you'll get in return is a blank stare. But if you press your face right up close to hers and contort it into grotesque shapes, she'll copy whatever you're doing. Stick out your

tongue, she'll stick out her tongue; open wide your mouth, and she'll open wide hers, too. Lacking anything else to do when we find ourselves thrown together, we do this, and the more we do it, the more I like her.

3. Her tendency to improve with age. Already Dixie has progressed from waking every ninety minutes and screaming at the top of her little lungs to waking every two hours and screaming at the top of her lungs. While this might seem insufferable to anyone who didn't know any worse, to me it seems like extraordinary progress. An act of goodwill, even. She still won't win any good citizenship awards, but she's gunning for Most Improved Player, and it's hard not to admire her for the effort.

But there's something else, too, which I hesitate to mention for fear it will be used against me the next time we divvy up the unpleasant chores around here. The simple act of taking care of a living creature, even when you don't want to, maybe especially when you don't want to, is transformative. A friend of mine who adopted his two children was asked by a friend of his how he could ever hope to love them as much as if they were his own. "Have you ever owned a dog?" he said. And that's the nub of the matter: All the little things that you must do for a helpless creature to keep it alive cause you to love it. Most people know this instinctively. For someone like me, who has heretofore displayed a nearly superhuman gift for avoiding unpleasant tasks, it comes as a revelation. It's because you want to hurl it off the balcony and don't that you come to love it.

THE FIRST RULE of fatherhood is that if you don't see what the problem is, you are the problem. For most of the past couple of weeks I hadn't been able to see what the problem was. Everything had been going swimmingly. For the first time since the birth of my second child I was able to get back properly to work. My fear that my children would starve, or, at the very least, be forced to attend public school, was receding. The time I needed to earn a living had to come from someplace, of course, but it hadn't been obvious to me where in the family it should come from. Not from my wife, to whom I am addicted. Not from my eldest child, who has made it clear that she can't survive on one minute less of parental attention than she received before her sister was born. The only person who would be perfectly untroubled by my absence was the baby. Having worked up enough feeling for her that I could say honestly that I preferred having her around to not, I could now, in good conscience, neglect her.

Sure enough, by laying Dixie off on her mother and various babysitters I was able to slip back into something like my old routine. Within a week I had a new book up and nearly running. All was well. And then her mother turned up in my office, with that look in her eye. I tried to head her off before she got started, by telling her just how secure I was making our family's finances. She was uninterested in the family's finances.

"You need to set aside time to spend with Dixie," she said.

"Oh," I said. "I've spent time with her."

"You just went an entire week without *seeing* her."

"It's not like she knows."

"*You* know," she said. Which was true. Sort of.

"How often do you want me to see her?"

"I think you should have enough material about Dixie to sustain a biweekly *Slate* column," she said.

My first thought was: *What kind of father is it who sees his child just enough to generate material for his column?* My second thought was: *My kind of father.*

In that spirit, but not only in that spirit, I took Dixie and her mother to the Parkway Theater in Oakland, to see *Italian for Beginners*. The Parkway Theater, the greatest invention since birth control, is a cinema that, on Monday nights, admits only people over the age of eighteen, and then only if they are accompanied by people under the age of one. Sixty parents of thirty babies purchase their tickets, order their dinners, gather their glow-in-the-dark dinner claim-check numbers, and head into a theater. There, seated on deep plush sofas, infants howling mightily all around them, relaxed for the first time in a week, they wait placidly for their dinners to arrive and their movie to begin. It usually does this without much warning. There aren't any previews or ads at the Parkway. Whatever they're showing just starts right up.

Watching a movie with thirty babies is different than watching a movie without them. It's actually better, in some ways. The babies themselves, all piled up in one place like that, are themselves worth paying to see. They tend to howl all at once—say, when a character laughs raucously or a shot rings out in the night. They also tend to sleep all at once—say, when a character isn't laughing or a shot isn't ringing out. Occasionally, they even perform amazing tricks. Just before the movie began, for instance, a six-month-old girl in the front row balanced herself in midair, with nothing for support but her father's unsteady palm. The whole crowd cheered.

The success of an evening at the Parkway turns on the movie. There are good movies to watch with babies and bad movies to watch with babies. *Italian for Beginners*, odd as it may sound to anyone who has seen it, turns out to be very nearly the perfect movie to watch with babies. It opens with a firm promise to be one of those bleak Scandinavian character pieces in which every character is either dying or despairing, or both.

This came as good news for us, as it seemed unlikely in the extreme that any character would laugh or that any shots would ring out in the night. Nobody needed murdering in this one. Also, there's nothing like the misery of life as presented in Scandinavian art to remind the new parent that, no matter how bad he thinks he has it, some people have it even worse. Scandinavians.

Without Dixie I would have stewed in my seat, thoroughly ticked off that I had been conned by the cheery-sounding title into sitting through an Ibsen drama. With Dixie I was pleased to have been conned.

But then something happened. Two things, actually. First, about midway through, a bleak Scandinavian character piece became a spoof on a bleak Scandinavian character piece. Everyone who needed to die died in a hurry, leaving the remaining characters to cope with their despair, unaided. And toward the end of the second act their quiet Nordic depression took a dangerous U-turn, as all at once they discovered, as if they were thinking an original thought, what Scandinavians have known for centuries: If you want to be happy in Scandinavia you have to go to Italy. The second thing that happened resulted directly from this shocking eruption of Scandinavian *joie de vivre*: Dixie woke up and began to holler.

The implicit rule at the Parkway is that you can let

your baby cry and enjoy the show and no one will think any less of you. The Parkway offers the guilt-relieving sensation usually available only to smokers who find themselves surrounded by other smokers or to fat people who find themselves seated on airplanes with other fat people. But if before you arrive at the Parkway you have earned a reputation with your wife as a neglectful father, this sensation is no longer so easily had. Instead, you must rise and walk around with your child until she is mollified. The final scenes of the movie I glimpsed only out of the corner of my eye. A happy Scandinavian remains, to me, an elusive sight.

THE OTHER NIGHT Quinn and I went camping in Fairyland. Fairyland is a toddler-sized Disneyland smack in the middle of Oakland. Three times each summer it sells tickets to about twenty-five parents and allows them to pitch their tents, and their toddlers, inside the park. For the first time in their young lives, twenty-five small children have a chance to spend the night under the stars or, at any rate, the skyscrapers that loom over Fairyland. A few months ago I mentioned to Quinn that we might do this, and she has been unable to contain herself on the subject ever since. Every other day she has asked me, "When are we going camping in Fairyland?" or "Can we sleep in a tent today?" She's never been camping or slept in a tent and can't possibly know what any of it means. That is why she wants so badly to do it.

We enter not through the main entrance but through a gate in the back of the place between the miniature Ferris wheel and the bumper boats. Twenty-five parents and their toddlers line up and wait for the gate to open so that they can rush in and find the softest, most level patch of grass to pitch their tents. In line are Quinn's friend Matts and his father, John. John is the reason

I am here; John told me about camping in Fairyland. John, who has done this once before, also told me that I didn't need to bring anything to Fairyland except a tent and sleeping bags: Fairyland would take care of the rest. But John, I notice, carries many more possessions than I do. I have only three large sacks; he has eight. What is in those other five sacks, I wonder? What does an experienced Fairyland camper bring with him that I have neglected to bring?

The gates swing open and the other families rush to find the best spots in the dish-shaped campground. Quinn is more interested in the fact that she appears to have Fairyland entirely to herself, and she rushes off past the Ferris wheel to pet the donkeys. The great thing about Fairyland, from the point of view of a three-year-old, is that it is designed with a thirty-six-inch-high person in mind. The horses on the carousel are designed for a thirty-six-inch-high person, the cars in the steam train are designed for a thirty-six-inch-high person, the long tunnel in the Alice-in-Wonderland section is designed for a thirty-six-inch-high person. It's a home explicitly for children between the ages of two and five; any ordinary seven-year-old is made to feel unwelcome. With one exception, it is a Lilliputian world drawn perfectly to scale. The exception is the donkeys. These large animals, which Quinn claims are "llamas," are also surprisingly aggressive. I rush after her and quickly lose any chance of securing a comfortable place to sleep. By the time I herd Quinn back into the saucer, all of the soft, level places have been taken. We'll be spending the night on the hard, steep slope just below the rim.

All the other fathers have their tents looking very tentlike. These are elaborate affairs, with great huge roofs and fancy walk-in entrances. The man in the tent beside me not only has his tent up and running, he has a fantastic contraption that looks like a giant fire extinguisher and sounds like a pneumatic pump. He's huffing and wheezing over the thing like a pro. He is inflating what appears to be a full-sized mattress inside his enormous tent. I do not own one of these. I have never even seen one of these. My tent is still in its sack on the ground.

Quinn looks around, then at me.

"Where is our tent, Daddy?"

"It's in there." I point to the blue sack.

"Why?"

"I haven't put it up yet. You want to help Daddy put up the tent?"

"I want to go see the llamas."

A bit tensely: "I need you to stay here while I put up our tent."

In a flash, she's gone.

One eye on the donkeys, I unravel the tent and count our possessions with the other. These are: the tent and two sleeping bags I bought last week at REI, one head-mounted coal miner's flashlight that Tabitha gave me so I could see the barbecue pit when I grilled at night, three diapers, one sack of wipes, a purple and green glow-in-the-dark toothbrush, one tube of strawberry-flavored toothpaste, insect repellant, a pair of what Quinn calls "my stripey PJs," along with the pink slippers she insisted she could not do without. Finally there is a tattered and yellowing Outward Bound student handbook from the last time I camped—years ago, when I spent a month wandering about a wilderness area in Oregon. In this tattered Outward Bound handbook is everything I have forgotten about camping. Or so I think. When I open it I see that it is, like Outward Bound itself, more concerned with my spiritual development than my survival. It's filled with aphorisms the Outward Bound student is meant to take to heart:

They are wet with the showers of the mountains,
and embrace the rock for want of a shelter.
—Job 24:8

For the first time in more than two decades, I pitch a tent. *It has such an odd shape to it*, I think to myself when I am finished. John wanders over and stares a bit. "It looks like one of those old Volkswagen beetles with a tarp thrown over it," he finally says.

"I'm a little worried the fly sheet isn't on right," I say.

He thinks about what appears to be my problem. "I think you'll be okay in downtown Oakland," he says.

The man in the tent next door continues to pump away at his inflatable mattress. Sweat drips from the tip of his nose. John leaves. I turn to the sweating man. So far as I can see, his giant inflatable mattress is no more inflated than it had been twenty minutes before. No longer does he seem quite the aficionado.

"What are you doing?" I ask.

He stops, relieved to have an excuse not to keep pumping away. "Trying to pump this fucking thing up," he says.

I peer into his tent at the limp mattress. "How does it work?" I ask.

"I'm not sure," he says. "My wife bought it." Pause. "This whole thing was my wife's idea."

I sympathize and yet at the same time do not. The truth is, I am pleased by his distress. It means that it is possible, just, that I am not the least-prepared father for the journey that lies ahead of us. Quinn and I may not survive, but we won't be the first to go.

A night in Fairyland divides fairly neatly into two dramatically different experiences. The first amounts to a rave for toddlers. The Fairyland staff lays out a buffet banquet of hamburgers, hot dogs, potato chips, and chocolate and vanilla cupcakes: food that not a single toddler can find anything to object to. Not a single vegetable! Not one fruit! For the first time since I have become a father I dine with my child, alongside other parents and their children, unaccompanied by torture-chamber shrieking. All the children eat happily, greedily, so that they can scramble away as quickly as possible to the Fairyland rides, which stay open until nine p.m. But there's more! At eight o'clock at night, when most of them would be in bed, they attend an expertly executed puppet show. They watch the story of Cinderella with giant sacks of popcorn on their laps and their mouths wide open. At eight-thirty a woman dressed as a gypsy leads them in song. At ten p.m. they stumble, exhausted and sated, back to their tents. There begins the second part of a night in Fairyland.

About two years ago, addled with lack of sleep, my wife and I adopted a firmish policy not to further encourage Quinn to view the middle of the night as the most interesting part of the day. We shut the door on her at nine p.m. and do our best not to hear or see her until seven in the morning. And it has worked, so far as we know, though she still tends to get up a few times a week around three a.m. and holler at the top of her lungs. But as a result of our policy I know next to nothing about her sleeping life. That changes this night.

We crawl into the tent at ten. For the next hour Quinn amuses herself by punching the roof and racing outside and trying to climb inside other people's tents. When even that gets old, she settles into her sleeping bag and instructs me to read her a book. Eleven-thirty at night must feel to a three-year-old like four in the morning to an adult, but Quinn lasts, along with every other child in the camp, until eleven-thirty. During the second reading of *Harold and the Purple Crayon*, she falls asleep. Here is a rough log of what occurs during the next six hours:

12:15. Quinn pokes me in the head until I wake up. "Wake up, Daddy. Wake up, Daddy," she says. "What?" I say. "I need you to snuggle me!" she says. I curl up next to her. She falls back to sleep.

1:00. "Daddy!" I wake up and find her seated bolt upright inside the tent. "What?" I say. "You forgot to put bug spray on me!" It's true. I apply insect repellant. She falls back asleep.

1:38. "My sleeping bag came off!" "What?" I say. "My sleeping bag!" she wails. I cover her up. "No!" she says. "I want *your* sleeping bag!" As her sleeping bag is four feet long, this presents a problem. We negotiate and compromise on both of us sleeping under both sleeping bags.

3:15. "An owl is in the tent!" Again, she's bolt upright. "What?" I say, scrambling for the miner's headlamp. By the time I find it, she's fast asleep.

4:12. "Daddy." I wake up. This time she's awake, alarmingly alert and rested. I am not. "What?" I ask. "Daddy, I just want to say how much fun I had with you today," she says. Actual tears well up in my eyes. "I had fun with you, too," I say. "Can we go back to sleep?" "Yes, Daddy." Then she snuggles right up against me for what I assume will be the long haul.

5:00. The fucking birds are actually chirping. Quinn, of course, awakens with them, turns to me, and begins to sing:

There was a farmer had a dog and Bingo was his
 name, O!
B-I-N-G-O
B-I-N-G-O
B-I-N-G-O
And Bingo was his name, O!

"It's still sleepy time," I mutter. "Is it time to wake up, Daddy?" "Not yet." Miraculously, she falls back to sleep.

5:45. It's still dark outside. I wake up to find Quinn standing in her pink slippers at our tent door, which she has unzipped. "Matts!" she shouts. "Are you awake?" I hear a cry from a distant tent: "Quinn. I'm awake! Are you awake?" "Matts!" shouts Quinn again. "I'm awake! I'm awake!"

Forty-five minutes later, the four of us are all stumbling off to a breakfast of Sugar Pops. John, if anything, looks worse than I feel. And yet neither of us feels deterred; the evening went pretty much as we'd expected. "I just heard that they do this at the Oakland Zoo," he says.

"When's that?" I hear myself saying.

THE SECOND RULE of fatherhood is that if everyone in the room is laughing, and you don't know what they're laughing about, they are laughing about you. A few months ago when I dropped Quinn off at school I had that peculiar fatherhood feeling of having just discovered in a crowded room that my fly was unzipped. From the moment I walked into her classroom, my mere presence seemed to remind her three lady teachers of some impossibly funny joke. They choked back giggles and turned away and pretended to be very busy organizing the dinosaurs in the sandbox and counting the graham crackers in the box. After a couple of days of this I finally asked one of them what was going on, and while she said, "Oh, nothing," she meant, "You don't want to know." But her smile was indulgent; whatever I had done evidently had caused no offense. I should have just let it drop. Instead, I sent in my wife to investigate.

"They wouldn't tell me exactly what it was," she said, when she'd returned from fetching Quinn from school. "But it has something to do with something Quinn said about your . . ."

"About my what?" I asked.

She looked pained.

"About my what?"

"About your penis."

"That's all you can tell me?"

"That's it."

That evening, as I showered, Quinn rushed into the bathroom. This in itself wasn't unusual. It's a hobby of hers to open the shower door and spray water all over the bathroom. She likes to watch her naked father wash the soap from his eyes with one hand and prevent a flood with the other. But this time she also had something she wanted to say.

"Daddy has a small penis!" she shouted.

The phrase came a bit too trippingly off her tongue. Clearly, it wasn't the first time she'd said it. I squinted down at her, menacingly, through soap bubbles.

"*What?*"

She took it up as a chant.

"Daddy has a small penis!

"Daddy has a small penis!

"Daddy has a small penis!"

As the little vixen spun out of control, I considered my options. To protest at all was to protest too much. I was as trapped as an elephant in quicksand or a politician in a gossip column. Anything I did or said in response would only make matters worse. Really, there were only two choices, silence or laughter, and so I laughed—

mainly because stoicism is impossible when your three-year-old daughter is hurling insults more or less directly at your privates. "Ha ha ha," I said, with what I hoped sounded like detached amusement. Sure enough, Quinn instantly lost interest in the whole subject.

Surprisingly quickly, my mere presence ceased to amuse her teachers. My vanity soon recovered, as it always does, and I'd very nearly forgotten all about the incident. But then, last week, as I walked through Quinn's classroom door, the giggles resumed.

I went straight to my wife.

"Yes, they're all laughing at you," she said. "But it's only because of the way you dress your daughter."

Since Dixie was born three months ago, it has been my job to dress Quinn. I had heretofore regarded my performance of this duty, and indeed any other duty I happen to perform, as little short of heroic.

"How do they know I dress her?" I asked.

"Because when you were out of town last week, I dressed her. And when she walked into school last week they all said, 'Mama must have dressed you today!' "

"What's wrong with how I dress her?"

"Oh, please."

"She looks fine when I dress her."

"She looks like a street person."

"Look," I said, pointing to Quinn's room. "There's a war in there every morning. I do the best I can."

"It's a war because she knows you don't know what you're doing."

You might think that I would have come away from this conversation relieved. It obviously could have been much, much worse. But a similar nerve had been struck, the one that is somehow more fully exposed in the male who must constantly defend his self and habits in a house of females. There was a time not very long ago when I didn't think twice of wearing the same hiking shorts for a week at a stretch, or even once of going a year wearing only the shirts that happened to be stacked on top. This was not sloth; this was not indolence; it was *efficiency*. A minute more spent dressing than was absolutely required was a minute wasted.

In the three months that her appearance has been my problem I have done my best to instill Quinn with the same ideals. "Daddy, I'm awake!" she screams at some bleak hour when she is the first in the house to rise. I stumble painfully over the barricades and into her room and throw clothes on her before she has a chance to wake up everyone else, too. It's true that I'm not thinking much about what clothes I'm throwing on her, but that's because *she's three years old*. She's not supposed to care how she looks, so long as she does not look wildly dissimilar to every other three-year-old. Plus, my theory is that so long as she's dressed to get dirty, the way small children are meant to, no one will notice that I haven't the first clue how to do her hair.

But a fact is a fact and I can't deny this one: In the past month or so, Quinn has become increasingly difficult for me to dress. Every morning for a month the first conversation I've had with her has sounded like this:

"Daddy, I want to wear a party dress."

"It's cold outside. Brrrrrrr! You should wear pants."

"I don't waaaaaaant toooo!"

"But I'm wearing pants!" (Spoken cheerily.)

"No! I hate you!"

With which she collapses howling in the corner of her closet, forehead pressed into the carpet like a Muslim at prayer. It's been an odd experience. Quinn has throughout this difficult period acquiesced happily to her mother's aesthetic judgment, but the moment I walk into her dressing room she revolts. If it's forty-five degrees and foggy, she insists on wearing a skimpy dress. If it's eighty degrees and sunny, she demands wool tights. When a day calls for pants and a T-shirt (as every day does, in my view), she calls for her hula-dancing costume and hollers until she gets it. By my lights, she is wildly unreasonable. By the lights of the women in her life, her mother and her teachers, she has finally and justifiably decided to resist my incompetence.

I have a tendency to prove, at least to myself, that whatever I happened to do in any given situation was exactly the right thing to have done. (Small penis syndrome, my wife now calls this.) This time, I surrender to a force greater than my opinion and try a new approach.

"I want to wear a party dress."

"Sure! Pick a dress!"

"Okay, Daddy! And Daddy, I want to wear Mama's lip gloss."

"Sure!"

"Great, Daddy!"

And from there it couldn't have gone more smoothly, except that the party dress hangs awkwardly, the lip gloss winds up as face paint, and her hair remains far outside my abilities to cope with. The truth is Quinn doesn't look any better than she did when I muscled her into pants and a T-shirt. The origin of vanity is not the desire to be admired by others but the need to be in charge. The other thing just follows from it.

I ONCE WENT to visit Roald Dahl at his home in the English countryside. The author of *Charlie and the Chocolate Factory*, *James and the Giant Peach*, and other macabre tales for children had just publicly denounced *The Satanic Verses* as an irresponsible piece of self-promotion. He didn't exactly endorse the fatwa that had just been issued against Salman Rushdie, but he came close, and I used this as an excuse to go and talk to him. He wasn't well—he was more or less confined to an upholstered chair and wasn't long for this world—but he could not have been better company. I remember next to nothing of what he said about Rushdie. What I recall was lunch. Several Dahls gathered, and a plate of ham cold cuts arrived at the table. Dahl said something about how closely the cold cuts resembled human flesh, and how he once thought of writing a story about children who are served cold cuts from the corpse of a missing friend. I expected someone at the table to complain, but instead his daughter giggled and told a story about how she had witnessed, firsthand, a butcher slice off his palm while running a shank of ham over a meat slicer. She went on to describe, to the delight of the entire family, how the slice of butcher's flesh fit perfectly on top of the stack of ham. Exactly like the ham we were about to eat! Sixty seconds into the meal the Dahls were vying to outgross each other with tales of severed limbs and pulsing pink flesh, while happily munching ham sandwiches. With the possible exception of Mrs. Dahl, the entire family had preserved into adulthood a child-like delight in the grotesque.

Once you have a small child you can see the full appeal of the Dahlian imagination. To a small child the adult world *is* grotesque. For a start, it's all ridiculously out of proportion: To a child every grown-up is a monster. Then there are all these events that occur in the grown-up world that a child, in trying to get her mind around them, distorts wildly. I went out of town on business last week. "Are you going on an airplane?" Quinn asked, before I left. "Yes," I said. "Are you going to an airport?" she asked. "Yes," I said. "Are they going to put chickens in your luggage?" she asked. I had to think about that one. Then it struck me: check-in luggage/ chickens in the luggage. How strange the adult world must seem when filtered through the child's vocabulary. Even those aspects of the adult world designed explicitly to give innocent pleasure to a child are often, to a child, either weird or downright horrifying. Which brings me to Mickey Mouse.

I had taken Quinn to a birthday party around the

corner from our house in Berkeley. The highlight of the birthday party was to be the appearance of Mickey Mouse. Mickey was meant to be kept a secret. The children would gather and play for a bit and then Mickey Mouse would burst through the doors and surprise everyone. But it's hard to keep a secret, especially a good one, from Quinn, as it is so tempting to use any prospective treat as a bribe. To coax her into her car seat I had told her that if she ceased to struggle she would get to meet Mickey Mouse. In the flesh. She seemed pleased by the idea.

We arrived at the birthday party. Quinn overcame the shyness she always experiences when she enters a crowded room and was soon playing with the other children. But there is no such thing as equilibrium in a room full of toddlers; something bad is always about to happen; and what happened was that the father of the birthday girl came over to say there was a problem with Mickey. The company that farmed out Mickey to children's birthday parties had just phoned: Mickey was ill. The company had called around looking for a substitute. They had found one, but he lived six hours away. He was on his way, but he'd be late.

You had to admire the commitment. In six hours you can get from our house in Berkeley to Reno, Nevada.

Some poor guy who lived, in effect, in Reno had tossed his Mickey Mouse costume in the trunk of his car in the wee hours of that morning and was now hauling ass across the country to humor a room full of three-year-olds. And he wasn't even the real Mickey Mouse. He was an understudy.

An hour or so later Quinn was off on one side of a large deck playing with a dollhouse. The other kids and adults mingled on the other side. I was munching a raw carrot and glancing across the deck every four seconds to ensure Quinn hadn't fallen off. Suddenly, onto the deck, between Quinn and everyone else, burst Mickey Mouse. He wore all the official gear. But still there was something off about him. In the first place, he wasn't alone. Trailing him was a ghoulish assistant, clutching balloons and sweating so profusely that one of the children turned to his mother and said, "Mommy, the man went swimming!" Together the two of them looked as if they had jogged, not driven, from Reno.

But the real problem was Mickey himself. He wasn't the cute little Mickey you think of when you think of Mickey Mouse. He was a large man, stuffed into a small costume that didn't quite fit. His giant mouse head tilted this way then that, as if partially severed. His white gloves failed to disguise the thick black hair on the backs of his hands. Even his black mouse slacks looked to be loaners; bending over hurriedly to greet the first child he saw, he flashed a rear, vertical smile. The first child he saw was Quinn.

I tried to imagine this scene from Quinn's point of view. The fact is that while she had pretended to be delighted that she was going to meet Mickey Mouse, she had never actually heard of the creature. God knows what she thought she was getting into, but it wasn't a six-foot rodent with a greaseball sidekick. Instantly—so quickly that Mickey didn't have a chance to lay his hairy mitts on her—her face dissolved in terror and she began to scream. Not a playful scream. A Janet Leigh in the shower in *Psycho* scream. I raced across the deck, clutched her in my arms, and spent the next five minutes consoling her. When she'd calmed down she squirmed away from me and ran into the house.

"Where are you going?" I hollered after her.

"To find Mickey Mouse!" she said.

For the next hour or so she enjoyed Mickey Mouse in a way that was new to me and I assume also to Mickey. Mickey Mouse, to Quinn, was not an endearing character. He was a serial killer. This was Disney with a twist of lime. She'd sneak right up to him and then, when he noticed her, dash away screaming bloody murder. It was strange to see. Her mother and father can't bear scary movies, and I'll bet money that when she grows up she won't like them, either. But in her current state of mind she likes nothing more than the toddler equivalent of a horror flick. If she weren't so much like every other small child, she'd be considered insane.

ONE OF THE many surprising things to me about fatherhood is how it has perverted my attitude toward risk. It is true that there are many kinds of risk—emotional, social, financial, physical. But I can't think of any I enjoy taking more than I did before I had children— unless you count the mere fact of having children as a kind of celebration of emotional risk. Otherwise, I'm rapidly becoming a wimp. There are little risk-averse things I do now that I never did before and little risk-averse feelings that I have now that I never had before. To wit:

Item: The other night Tabitha and I went to see *Minority Report*. It's the sort of movie that just a few years ago I would have cheered and Tabitha would have at least tolerated. But in the middle of the film a small child is abducted from a public swimming pool. That was enough to ruin it for Tabitha and to make me feel we ought to just skip dinner afterward and go home and make sure nothing terrible had happened to *our* children. This is obviously neurotic. I don't know a single case of a small child being kidnapped at a public swimming pool in Berkeley, California, while her father holds his breath underwater, much less from her bed at night while being guarded by babysitters. But I am no longer rational on this subject. My emotions are easily manipulated by cheap dramatic tricks involving the suffering of small children, and by the current media hysteria about what is in fact an ordinary rate of child murders. I think I could still sit through the scene in *Richard III* when the villain has the two little princes smothered in their beds. Anything closer to twenty-first-century American life ruins my day.

Item: I no longer enjoy rolling the dice in the stock market. I never enjoyed it all that much, but what pleasure I took in it vanished with Quinn's arrival—well before the stock market collapsed. With her arrival, for the first time in my life, I began to worry a bit about money. I have no reason to worry about money, but that doesn't stop me from doing it. When people talk about the mood in the financial markets they tend to assume that the market drives that mood. But of course it doesn't, not entirely. A few years ago a piece in the *Michigan Medical Journal* argued that the reason the Internet bubble reached such ridiculous heights was that huge numbers of investors were now taking drugs that lowered their inhibitions. With a third of the U.S. investing population on Prozac or some other mood-enhancing drug, the paper concluded, it was no wonder that so many people believed the market would simply keep rising.

Small children are also a mood-altering substance with financial consequences. Their effect on the human mind is the opposite of Prozac. At any rate, my own current financial taste for cash and bonds seems to be at least partly a response to parenthood.

Item: I am no longer as open as I once was to helping out people I don't know, especially when those people need a bath. Several times a week I have a vaguely hostile response to a stranger that I would not have had if I didn't have children—for instance, when I see a bum loitering in the park near our house. I find it less amusing than I once did when people knock on my front door to ask me to join some religion or sign some petition. I used to pick up hitchhikers every now and again, but I wouldn't think of doing it today. In general, the probability that I will extend myself to a stranger in need, always slight, is now zero.

Item: Not long after our first child was born, but well before September 11, 2001, I began to experience a mild fear of flying. There was a time in my life when I could, fairly blithely, hop out of an airplane with a parachute on my back; now I can't get onto an airplane without melodramatic feelings of doom. When I travel, I carry pictures of my children for the sole purpose of having one long look at them the moment after the engine dissolves into flames and the plane enters its final dive. These occasional spasms of terror are as pathetic as they are undeniable. The only explanation I can come up with—other than that I've become a pussy—is that I can now imagine an elaborate narrative triggered by my tragic death. Before I had children I had no particular reason to fear dying, because I had no particular notion of the consequences of my death. If I had died in some absurd accident it wouldn't have mattered all that much. Now, because of the children who would be left without a father and the wife who would be left alone to care for them, my life seems more important, even though, in some respects, it is actually much less important (having, as I do, fewer years to lose).

I am aware that all these feelings are more or less nuts. But they are also more or less true. I know for a fact that my children are insane. Or, at any rate, I know that if an adult behaved as my children do, he would be institutionalized. Is it possible that they are contagious?

WHEN I CAME to, the first thing I noticed was that wherever I was, I had never been there before. Flat on my back, an oxygen mask on my face, I looked up and saw a silver wall, some flashing lights, and a man in a dark blue jumpsuit, his back to me. The mask made it hard to call out. I tried to raise my arm but couldn't. My arms and my legs were strapped down. My head, too. My gaze was directed straight down at my bare chest and the several wires taped to it. My stomach, I could see, was caked with blood. My khakis, too, were a dull dry red. On the left side of my face I felt the warm pleasant drip-drip-drip of even more blood. Apparently, I'd been in some sort of accident: What sort? I had no idea. But I knew what I was meant to do, from TV shows. I wiggled my fingers, then my toes.

The man in the blue suit turned around and removed my oxygen mask. I now realized, again from TV shows, that I was in the back of an emergency rescue unit.

"I can feel my toes and fingers," I reported knowingly.

"What's your name?" he asked.

I told him. But my voice sounded strange and manufactured, not my natural own.

"That's good, Michael," he said, and smiled with a terrifying condescension. This man knew something I didn't: What?

"Do you know what day it is?" he asked.

"I never know what day it is," I said.

"He says he never knows what day it is," he said. Out of the corner of my eye I now spotted a second man in a dark blue emergency rescue uniform. And I remembered something: Quinn on an ice rink. I remembered skating over to her awkwardly, like a man pumping a Razor scooter up a steep hill, and then skating back to my own beginner's ice-skating lesson. I also remembered that they had lumped the beginners together with the intermediates. I remembered a short, squat Irishman showing me how to spin. I recalled thinking: *If I try to spin I'll kill myself.* But what I couldn't remember was why I was ice-skating in the first place.

"Do you know your address?"

I did, just.

"Michael, you've been a little funny for some time."

I now recalled why I was ice-skating. I was ice-skating because Quinn's mother had conceived that the three of us should do something meaningful together. Just one thing, to remind Quinn that she was still special. We cast about for one meaningful thing and landed upon ice-skating. Tabitha knew how to ice-skate, Quinn and I did not. Quinn and I would learn together, side by side. In that briefly harmonious spirit we had set off, presumably not long before, for the local ice rink. What I couldn't remember was why we needed to remind Quinn she was special.

"Where are my wife and daughter?" I asked.

"They're outside in your car," he said. "Do you remember what kind of car you have?"

I did, a bit more clearly. "How long have I been unconscious?" I asked. He didn't answer.

"What year is it?" he asked. A wave of irritation crashed over me. My head pounded. I didn't care what year it was, or what car I owned, or what I had eaten for dinner. I had bigger problems. Such as: Who was I? Or rather: Was I the same me as I had been before whatever had happened to me happened to me? I needed for the man to sit down and listen to my life story, from the beginning, to see if it all felt familiar. Then I remembered something else: the book! Before I fell on my head, I was writing a book.

"Can you remember what year it is?" asked the emergency rescue worker.

I told him what year it was. This time the answer came to me easily.

"Do you remember falling?"

"No."

"What do you remember?"

"I remember that if I don't hand in my book in six weeks, I'm fucked."

He looked at me a little strangely. "Okay," he said. "That's a start."

And so I told him about my literary problems. How thrilling it had been to be handed material so rich that I was limited only by my ability to handle it. How for months I'd been haunted by the sense that something would interfere with my finishing it. How, a few months earlier, with about a third of the book done, the manuscript had been stolen, along with everything I had ever written and not published, including fifteen years of private journals and biographies I had kept of my two daughters. How a fancy truck with darkened windows—it was spotted by a neighbor—had rolled up alongside my office in broad daylight. How its occupants had picked the lock to my office, stolen my computer, all my backup files (from a separate room), and . . . nothing else. How they'd left no fingerprints, only a mystery.

Then, by some miracle of brain chemistry, I realized I sounded like a lunatic. "I know this sounds nuts," I said.

"This all happened?"

"This all happened," I said.

I explained to the man—who continued to stare calmly at me; how, I do not know—how my wife had understood, or pretended to, that to compensate for the loss of my manuscript I needed to abandon most of my responsibilities as a father. How I had spent several months redefining what is meant by "the bare minimum"—how little a husband and father can do and still not trigger screams of terror when he walks in the front door. How I had a genius for it—and an excuse. A deadline. How Dixie didn't seem to mind—a father doesn't add much to the life of a six-month-old child—but that Quinn was different. The moment I put some space between me and her, she set about trying to drive her mother insane. She'd eat nothing but sugar, do nothing but watch cartoons. Denied sugar and cartoons, she took to calling her mother "you stupid lady." Told not to talk to her mother that way, she'd spit, absurdly, "Jack-n-ass!" Somewhere in there she got her first bad report card: Her teacher said that the normally ebullient Quinn was now, occasionally, "morose." On my brief visits home I saw more truculence than moroseness, but that was as alarming, in its way. On Christmas morning, the moment she realized that she'd ripped open her last present she looked up and said, "Oh, shit." *Fucking hell*, I thought, *where did that come from?*

When I spoke that last line the ambulance man laughed. "He's okay," he shouted out to his colleague. They changed their plan to drive me to the trauma center to determine if I'd suffered brain damage. Instead, they would drive me to the emergency room to have my head sewn up. Before they did, they invited Tabitha into the truck to tell me that she and Quinn would be right behind me, in the aforementioned car. My wife is at her best in such moments; she's as good in a crisis as ice on a burn. After making it clear to me that I was a wimp to be concerned about the state of my brain, she said that I didn't need to worry about Quinn: She had hustled her off the ice before she could see her father lying in a lake of blood. It's astonishing how much trouble we take to prevent our children from seeing the world as it is. It's even more astonishing how, even when we might think we have earned a right to forget about our children for a moment, we haven't.

The ambulance started, the siren wailed. I remembered another thing: Quinn needed to feel special because I had spent too much time working on my book. I was learning how to ice-skate because someone had broken into my office and stolen my book. The theft of my computer memory had led to this assault on my own.

The emergency rescue worker was back to fiddling with one of the machines hooked up to me. He seemed to think we were done talking. We weren't. My mind wasn't right, and I knew it wasn't right. I thought:

When you hit your head and you are never again the same, how do you know? If you have that thought does that mean you are the same? I didn't know; and I was certain the only way I would know was to talk and talk and talk. "I've got to finish this book soon," I said, a little desperately.

"Uh-huh," he said.

"No," I said, "I still have a problem."

"Yeah?"

"I can't remember what the book's about."

"Give me a moment," he said. He didn't even try to hide it: I was boring him. I was boring the emergency rescue worker! I must have fallen asleep, as the next thing I knew I was looking up not at an emergency rescue worker but a lady doctor. "I hear you're a writer," she said, making conversation. "What do you write about?"

She was soon sorry she had asked. For it was then I remembered: Baseball! I was writing a book about baseball. As she stitched me back together I offered her, free of charge, my literary autobiography. Every last detail, including the occasional journal I'd been keeping of my family life. I told her, for instance, I'd written about the birth of my child, which had occurred in this very hospital. I told her I'd lived in Paris, and published some accounts of the experience. It was then that she perked up.

"I read those!" she said.

Inexplicably, I felt better.

"I loved those descriptions of you with your son in the Luxembourg Gardens."

"That was Adam Gopnik," I said. For the first time I felt something I knew I had always felt. The surge of irritation, the choking back of indignation—oh, the horror, oh, the smallness of existence—was so breathtakingly familiar that I couldn't deny it: I was still me.

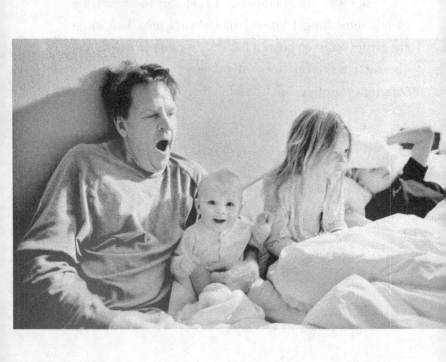

PART 3

WALKER

TWO HAD SEEMED like the right number to both of us until we had two, and even then it seemed sort of like the right number to me. Two was always the plan; five years ago, at fantastic expense, with the view to maximizing our living space while giving each child her own room, we'd torn up a four-bedroom house and made it into a three-bedroom house. Then one day Tabitha began to shoot me long, soulful looks at night and say things like, "I just feel like someone's missing." She thought we should at least discuss the idea of having a third child, but of course all that meant was that

she'd already made up her mind. It was up to me to prevent it, which is to say that it was only a matter of time
before it happened. And that was that. Tabitha called
the architect who had torn out the fourth bedroom, and
told him we'd be building an addition.

Beep! Beep! Beep!

To the shriek of an alarm I awaken but don't move.
What with the extra pillow and the warm blanket, the delivery room couch had proved surprisingly
comfortable.

Beep! Beep! Beep!

Having witnessed childbirth twice before, I have
acquired this expertise: I know that alarms on delivery
room machines are nothing to fear. Along with smoke
detectors and airport security machines, they belong on
the long list of devices in American life designed to cry
wolf. Apart from that, here is the sum total of what I've
learned waiting for my children to be born: (1) *arrive
sober*; (2) do not attempt to be interesting, as it makes
the nurses uneasy; (3) never underestimate your own
insignificance; and (4) try to get some sleep, as no one
else can. Of course, it is important to be present and
conscious for the birth of your child. To miss it would
be to invite scorn and derision and lead others to speak
ill of you behind your back. But up until the moment
the child is born, the husband in the delivery room is in

an odd predicament. He's been admitted to the scene of the crisis but given no serious purpose. He's the Frenchman after the war resolution has passed.

I had just pressed a second pillow hard over my head to mute the alarm—it sounded as if it might be coming from the painkiller pump—and was very nearly asleep, when I heard a new voice. "You're ten centimeters," it said.

The last time they'd brought the chains out onto the field, they'd measured her at a mere four centimeters. Ten was clearly forward progress, but it had been nearly five years, and I couldn't recall how many centimeters there were in a first down. I rose on the couch, and in the unnaturally bright tone of a man pretending he hasn't just been asleep, asked, "So . . . how many more centimeters we got to go?" That's when I noticed we had a new doctor. She looked at me strangely. "Ten centimeters means the baby's coming," she said.

"Oh."

She'd been in the room only a couple of minutes, as it turned out. Before that, Tabitha had never seen or heard of her and—as the doctor now mentions—she's about to quit delivering babies and move to Detroit, so this is likely to be the extent of our relationship. "I'm Dr. Vay," she says, and grabs a stool and a mask. It's 4:23 in the morning and the mood in the air, as far as I'm concerned, is giddy exhaustion. "Oy vey!" I holler as Dr. Vay moves into the catching position. Only somehow it comes out, "Ai vay!"

"It's oy vey, honey," Tabitha says calmly. "Can you get the mirror?"

I find the mirror. In Berkeley, no birth is complete without a mirror. The belief here is that the mother, as she grunts and groans, should have all five senses fully engaged and pumping meaning into the experience. The ideal Berkeley birth has probably never actually happened, but if it has, it happened far from civilization, in the woods, without painkillers or doctors or any intervention whatsoever by modern medicine. Along one side of the birthing mother was a wall of doulas wailing a folk song; along the other, all the people she had ever known; at her feet, a full-length mirror, in which she watched her baby emerging; at her head, a mother wolf, licking and suckling. Incense-filled urns released meaningful, carbon-free odors. The placenta was saved and, if not grilled, recycled.

Tabitha never wanted the full Berkeley. But back when we started, seven and a half years ago, she gave a passing thought to employing a midwife instead of a doctor, and thought that it might make the experience more meaningful if she skipped the painkillers. She picked out music and found scented oils with which to be rubbed. To the immense irritation first of her obstetrician and then of herself, she hired a doula, who was meant to use said oils to massage her feet during the delivery, but instead went out for turkey sandwiches and never came back.

That was seven and a half long years ago. With her slender build and narrow hips and near-total intolerance of physical discomfort, my wife was ill-designed for childbirth. The first time around, in this very hospital, she began to hemorrhage. The doctors saved her life, and with so little drama that we didn't realize what they'd done until well after. The second time around, again in this hospital, they saved not only her but our second daughter, who had entered the birth canal at a historically tragic angle. Entering her third pregnancy, my wife lost interest in doulas and incense. She longs only for painless, antiseptic, impersonal modern medicine. Numb is good. If they ran tubes underground from hospitals to homes so that painkillers could be delivered in advance of labor, she might well have been their first paying customer. Of the original Berkeley Dream, the mirror's all she's got left.

"Can you feel the contractions happening?" the doctor asks.

"Slightly." She's lying, thank God. If she felt a thing she'd be hollering.

Beep! Beep! Beep! The painkiller pump, again. Another nurse appears—another stranger we're almost surely never again to lay eyes upon. "Angie needs a break," she says. Angie's the nurse who still hasn't worked out what's going wrong with the painkiller. Angie exits. Dr. Vay prods and pushes and massages and waits. Behind her on the wall is a small sign, bearing the first words my child will see: *We Strive to Give Five Star Service.*

"I think you're having one now. Push."

Tabitha pushes, turns beet-red, and goes all bug-eyed.

"Maybe you shouldn't hold your breath," I say helpfully. No one notices. A single thirty-minute nap and I've lost what little right I had to be heard.

"Can you feel anything at all?" the doctor asks.

"Not really."

"Imagine you're trying to poop," says the doctor.

Worried that imagining might make it so, I retreat up and away from ground zero, and stroke the tippy-top of my wife's head. But this just further isolates me as the character in search of a role—the carrot in the school play. Out of nothing more than a desire to seem busy, I grab hold of one of Tabitha's legs and pull it backward. Then, like the master on a slave ship counting the strokes, I begin to chant. "One, two, three . . ." I half expect the doctor and nurses to fall about laughing and tell me to stop, but they don't. I seem, in fact, to have written myself a speaking part. "One! Two! Three! One! Two! Three!" Tabitha pushes harder. Her eyes look as if they are about to pop out of her head and ricochet off the ceiling.

"Here it is."

There comes a moment when I cease to be able to watch the birth of what is presumably my child with anything but horror. This is that moment. It's meant to be a beautiful sight—a thing to be videotaped or at least remembered, and played over and again in the mind— but it feels more like a hideous secret to be kept. But the damn mirror makes it hard to avoid. Ten minutes ago there was no place to hide; now there is no place to look.

Boy or girl? We didn't know. But girls were all we'd ever done, and we'd spent a lot less time arguing over boys' names than girls'. She'd gone from Clementine to Penelope to Phoebe to Scout and then back to Penelope. At midnight when the water broke all over the living room floor, we were just starting what I assumed would be a long creep back to Clementine. I liked the sound of Penny Lewis, but Clementine made you want to sing.

"That's the best push yet!" says the doctor. "One more time."

"One, two, three . . ." I feel like Richard Simmons in one of his videos. *You can do it!*

"One more just like that."

"One! Two! Three!"

Next comes the sound of a hairless dog escaping from quicksand. *Sluuuuuuuurrrrppp!*

"It's a boy!"

And with that, Walker Jack Lewis comes into the world.

ONCE THEY WHEEL Tabitha from the delivery room to the recovery room, Stage 1 ends and Stage 2 begins. For the whole of Stage 1, a father performs no task more onerous than seeming busy when he isn't. Nothing in Stage 1 prepares him for Stage 2, when he becomes, in a heartbeat, chauffeur, cook, nurse, gofer, personal shopper, Mr. Fixit, sole provider, and single parent. Stage 2 is life as a Mexican immigrant, with less free time. Entering Stage 2, I know from experience, I have between twenty-four and forty-eight hours before I'm overwhelmed by a tsunami of self-pity. I set out to make the most of them.

The first assignment is to fetch our seven- and four-year-old daughters from home so that they can meet their new baby brother and see firsthand the joy of partial disinheritance. The birth is supposed to have put them into a delicate psychological state. As I enter the house, I see no trace of it, however, or, for that matter, of them. Just inside the front door lies the shrapnel from an exploded giant Reese's Peanut Butter Cup. In the kitchen is the residue of what seems to have been a pancake breakfast for twenty. Dishes long banished from use have migrated out of the backs of kitchen cabinets, toys untouched for years litter their bedroom floors. Exactly thirteen hours ago, at midnight, our kind and generous next-door neighbors left their own bed for ours, so that we might go to the hospital and have a baby. Briefly, I have the feeling that if I turned around and walked away, my children would very happily use these new grown-ups to create a new life for themselves and never think twice about it.

At length, I find them, at play with their benign overlords in the courtyard. "Daddy! Daddy! Daddy!" they shriek.

We embrace histrionically. They know where I've been, and they know their mother has given birth. But instead of asking the obvious question—to what?—they race off to find various works of art they've created in the past six hours. "You have a baby brother!" I shout at their vanishing backs. A baby brother, as it happens, is exactly what they both claimed to least want. "A baby brother!" they shriek.

I've never been able to feel whatever it is I'm meant to feel on great occasions, so I shouldn't expect them to, either. But of course I do. It's not until they climb into the minivan that they finally get a grip. "Daddy?" asks Dixie, age four, from her seat in the third row. "How does the baby get out of Mama?"

This minivan is new. I've never been in the same

car with a person who still seemed so far away. In the rearview mirror, her little blond head is a speck.

I holler back what little I know.

"Daddy?" asks Quinn, age seven.

"Yes, Quinn."

"How do cells get from your body into Mama's body?"

We wheel into the hospital parking lot.

"Help me look for a parking spot."

That distracts her: They love to look for parking spots. In the Bay Area, looking for parking spots counts as a hobby. One day when they are grown, their therapists will ask them, "What did you and your father do together?" and they will say, "Look for parking spots."

We find a spot and instantly the race is on to the hospital elevators, followed by the usual battle-to-the-death to push the up/down button, followed by the usual cries from Dixie that because Quinn pushed the up/down button she has first dibs on the floor button, followed by Quinn's usual attempt to push the floor button, too. Since not long after Tabitha began to balloon, they've treated every resource as scarce; one of anything has become *casus belli*; no object is too trivial to squabble over. A Gummi Worm vitamin, for instance, or a ripped pair of stockings. Produce in their presence an actually desirable object—an elevator button in need of punching or, God forbid, a piece of candy—and you'll have screams inside of a minute and tears inside of two. Oddly enough, they used to get along.

When the elevator doors open onto the third floor—all smiles, you'd never know how narrowly they'd just averted bloodshed—they come face to knee with Shirley. Shirley is the large and intimidating security guard assigned to prevent the twelve thousand babies born each year in the Alta Bates hospital from being stolen. She must be a success at it, as she's been guarding them even longer than we've been making them. This is the very same Shirley who, seven and a half years ago, prevented Quinn from being abducted at birth, and thus spared some poor kidnapper years of sleep deprivation.

But even Shirley presents the girls with no more than a small speed bump in their endless race. Security badges gleefully grabbed, they resume their competition to see who will be the first to find Mama's room, Number 3133. Advantage Quinn, again, as Dixie can't read any number greater than ten. With Dixie behind her running as fast as her little legs will carry her and screeching, "Wait for me, Quinn!" Quinn flies to her mother's hospital door. And there, amazingly, she stops in her tracks. The big, cold recovery room door is too much for even her to barrel through. She knocks nervously and announces her presence, giving Dixie just time enough to catch up.

"Just let me put some clothes on!" I hear Tabitha shout.

That's not what she's doing. She's setting the stage.

Much effort, none of it mine, has gone into preparing for this moment. She's bought and read them countless books about sibling rivalry; taken them to endless sibling prep classes at the hospital; rented many sibling-themed videos narrated by respected authorities—*Dora the Explorer* for Dixie, *Arthur* for Quinn; watched with them, every Sunday night, their own old baby videos; and even bought presents to give to them *from the baby* when they visit him in the hospital. Before this propaganda blitz, our children may or may not have suspected that they were victims of a robbery, but afterward they were certain of it. Hardly a day has passed in months without melodramatic suffering. One afternoon I collected Dixie from her preschool—to take one of approximately six thousand examples—and learned that she'd moped around the playground until a teacher finally asked her what was troubling her. "When the baby comes, my parents won't love me as much," she'd said. Asked where she'd got that idea from, she said, "My big sister told me."

I've sometimes felt that we're using the wrong manual to fix an appliance—that, say, we're trying to repair a washing machine with the instructions for the lawn mower. But my wife presses on, determined to find room enough for three children's happiness. The current wisdom holds that if you seem to be not all that interested in your new child the first time the older ones come to see him, you might lessen their suspicion that he's come to pick their pockets. And so that's what she's doing in there: As her children wait at her hospital door, she's moving Walker from her bed into a distant crib.

"Okay, come in!"

They push through the door and into the room.

"Can I hold him, Mom?" asks Quinn.

"No, I want to hold him!" shouts Dixie.

And with that Walker's identity is established: one of something that we need two of. In less time than it takes an Indy pit crew to change a tire, Quinn's holding him and Dixie's waiting her turn, swallowing an emotion she cannot articulate and wearing an expression barely distinguishable from motion sickness.

THERE IS A warning sign before the trouble begins, but I miss it. The afternoon I bring Tabitha home from the hospital is also the day of our neighbor's glamorous wedding, in which Quinn and Dixie are to be the flower girls. In walks Tabitha, and off flounce her little girls with other grown-ups to the Mark Hopkins Hotel, to have their hair and makeup done, and then lead a bride to her doom. *Good*, I think, *the little monsters are gone for the day, and Tabitha will have one day of peace in the house, before the war resumes.* But when I deliver Mother's Milk Tea to her in bed, I find her sobbing. "I just wanted to be there when our little girls walked down the aisle," she says, as if they, not our neighbor, were getting married. This is unusual; her mind has a slight tendency to race to some tragic conclusion, but she usually stops it before it arrives. I hug her, pretend to sympathize, tell her that it's no big deal to miss just one of approximately three thousand occasions on which her little girls will dress up like princesses and preen in public. And she appears to agree, and to feel better. *Fixed that one*, I think, and move on to the next. A family is like a stereo system: A stereo system is only as good as its weakest component, and a family is only as happy as its unhappiest member. Occasionally that is me; more often it is someone else; and so I must remain vigilant, lest the pleasure of my own life be dampened by their unhappiness.

On this first night, even after the girls return, it is not. I can't believe it: Five people in the room and there is nothing wrong with any of them. I'm like a man who has fallen from a ten-story building only to get up and walk away without a scratch. I'd count all my blessings, but I'd run out of fingers, so I stick with the big ones. For the first time in three attempts, my wife has given birth without needing doctors to save the child's life or hers. She's so physically robust that she declined a second free night in the hospital and came home early. Our baby is healthy and—a first in my experience of newborns—reasonable. He cries when he's hungry and weeps before he farts and otherwise appears to be satisfied with the world as he finds it. Even his older sisters have gone into remission. Eight hours of the full princess treatment distracts them for a few more from their suspicion that a new baby brother means less of everything for them. We spend an hour in front of the fire like a fairy-tale family, listening to them relive their first wedding. "When we walked down the aisle, they played Taco Bell's Canyon," Quinn says knowingly. (Named for its German composer, Johann TacoBell.)

When they're done, they yawn and go off to bed, sweetly, like fairy-tale children, and leave us with fairy-tale leisure—which we use to decode this year's Christmas cards, stacked up and waiting for weeks. There's the drummer in the rock band who sends us a card each year but each year has got himself an entirely new family. Not merely a new wife but, seemingly, new cousins, aunts, and uncles. Who are they? There's a couple we've never seen, apart from in the picture they've helpfully included, but who say how nice it was to get together with us not once but twice in 2006. Who are *they*?

Two happy little girls sleep in their bunks, and a new baby boy sleeps in the contraption Tabitha has rigged up beside our bed—having given away the expensive co-sleeper she swore we'd never again need because she was done having babies. In time she joins him, and so I curl up with Malthus's *An Essay on the Principle of Population*, a new edition for which, oddly enough, I owe an introduction. "I think I may fairly make two postulates," writes Malthus, before advancing the most famously wrong prediction about humanity ever made. "First, That food is necessary to the existence of man. Secondly, That the passion between the sexes is necessary and will remain nearly in its present state." And off he sets, with the cool hysteria of the Unabomber's manifesto, to argue that my biggest problem circa 2007 should be a shortage of corn. On the other side of the Bay, fireworks explode. It's New Year's Eve.

Just before two in the morning, I'm prodded awake. It's Tabitha, with a look on her face I've never seen there before. "I'm sorry," she says.

"Okay," I say. "What's the matter?" But I already know it's serious. She's fighting very hard to hold it together. Her eyes dart around, and she fidgets as if she itches in fifty places at once.

"I don't know," she says, "I'm really, really scared."

She's like an addict in need of a fix that does not exist. She's terrified. Worse, she doesn't know what she's terrified of. All she knows is that she can't be alone, can't even close her eyes in my presence without shuddering with fear. "I think I might need to go to the emergency room," she says reluctantly, and she might. But it's two in the morning, we have three small children in the house, the neighbors are all gone, and the nearest blood relation is two thousand miles away.

"Tell me exactly what you feel."

"As if something really bad's going to happen."

Tears fill her eyes.

"I feel like I don't have any control of anything. I feel like I might be going insane."

Five minutes later I'm leaving messages on doctors' voice mails with one hand and Googling with the other:

Childbirth. Panic.

At the top pops alternative translations of Psalm 48:6 (*Panic seized them there, / Anguish, as of a woman in childbirth*). Skipping down, I find what appears to be a relevant entry: *Post-traumatic Stress Disorders After Childbirth.*

"Have you ever heard of this?" I ask her.

"No," she says. But then a lot of unpleasant things can happen to a woman after childbirth, and you don't hear about most of them until they happen to your wife in the middle of the night.

"Don't leave me alone," she says, trembling beside me.

I don't think I've ever seen her scared of anything, and she is now more frightened than I've ever seen another human being outside of the movies. She's the little kid in *The Sixth Sense*. She sees dead people. Still, born with the ability to remain calm in the face of other people's misery, I feel more curious than alarmed. People who actually are going insane don't know they are going insane. Googling on, I finally come to a plausible-sounding Web page written by a psychiatrist named Christine Hibbert. "Three common fears experienced by women with a Postpartum Panic Disorder are: 1) fear of dying, 2) fear of losing control, and/or 3) fear that one is going crazy."

It's like finding the picture of the red-throated
diver in the bird-watching manual right after you've
glimpsed one for the first time. *Postpartum Panic Disorder*: So now the thing has a name. Roughly one woman
in ten experiences it after childbirth. How, then, could
we never have heard of it?

At length a doctor calls back: Stay with her, she says,
and do what you can to calm her down. But she may
become completely hysterical, in which case she'll need
to go to the hospital.

The next six hours offer a new experience. She can't
sleep; she can't close her eyes for fear of her mind thinking some terrible thought. But I know—or think I know,
which amounts to the same thing—that she's suffering
from some chemical glitch that would repair itself in
time and that a pill would fix instantly. What she feels
has nothing to do with who she is. It's a state of mind
triggered by an event that she will never again endure.
She might just as well have turned bright green for a
day. But she doesn't know this. She's sure as Malthus
that this terror is going to be with her forever—and yet
she's as brave as she can be about it. Amazingly, the only
thing that makes her feel better is me. I fix her tea, rub
her back, and try to enjoy being the sane one for as long
as it lasts.

ONE AFTERNOON I find my wife standing in the kitchen preparing, once again, to cry. The pills they gave her instantly silenced the brain screams. She's gone from being terrified that she's losing her mind and that everyone she loves is going to soon die to being, occasionally, sad. I'll come across her getting dressed or sterilizing baby bottles, standing as still as a lady in a Vermeer painting, with tears in her eyes. There's no point in asking what's the matter—you might as well ask a flat tire why it doesn't have air. She's enduring this strange hormonal postpartum deflation that has nothing, really, to do with her. She's gone from needing to be rescued to wanting to be comforted. Which is, in theory, where I come in.

On the afternoon in question, the girls snack on tubes of yogurt, which they will now eat only if they come frozen just so—even though they aren't meant to be frozen. I walk in, note them squabbling madly about who gets the grape yogurt and who the strawberry, see the pools growing in Tabitha's eyes, take her in my arms, and ask, "Do you two have any idea how lucky you are to have a mom who takes such good care of you?"

Dixie, preoccupied with the Battle for the Grape One,

does not hear me, but Quinn looks up for a moment, stares at us, and says, "There's lots of good moms."

It's her new trick, to render cold and dispassionate judgments about her parents at their moments of greatest vulnerability. Two days earlier she and Dixie were both home sick, and I went off to my office, consumed with anxiety, to figure out (a) how expensive it was going to be to build another bedroom for the baby (very), and (b) how I was ever going to work again when I didn't sleep. At the first opportunity Quinn snuck into the TV room, clicked around the TiVo, found a biography of Bill Gates, and called Dixie in to watch it with her. An hour later I returned to find them both waiting for me: Quinn with hands on hips, Dixie forlorn and grasping a handful of berries.

"Daddy," said Dixie seriously. "I got some berries from the Gulf Stream waters."

"Why did you do that?"

"So we can eat them. Because we are poor."

Which seemed like a sweet reaction to the Bill Gates documentary, until Quinn fixed me with her I'm-here-to-speak-the-truth-to-power stare and said, "We're poor, Daddy. And you didn't tell us. You lied to us."

As always, it's hard to say whether it's developmental or just mental. Must the seven-year-old mind discover for itself every possible way to offend other people before it can settle on a more sociable approach? Is this just the bug that comes with the software upgrade? I don't know. At any rate, as I stand there with her mother crying in my arms searching for the words that will encourage her to be sweet, I come up empty. "Your mother takes really good care of you and me and Dixie and Walker, and I'm really proud of her," I finally say.

"You're just saying that to make her feel better," says Quinn.

Just four weeks after the birth of my son, both of my daughters are living, in effect, outside the law. They act as if they have nothing to lose, and, materially speaking, they don't. They've behaved so badly, for so long, that everything that might be taken away from them has been taken away: TV, candy, desserts, playdates, special dinners, special breakfasts, special outings with parents. They are like a pair of convicts in a Soviet gulag with nothing more than they need to survive—and still they continue to subvert the authorities. Oddly, their teachers all say that at school they remain little angels.

One evening it's just me and the little angels at the dinner table. Tabitha nurses Walker in another room. I have just tried, and failed, to settle the tenth dispute of the evening—who will sit in which seat—with a coin flip. At first they loved this new approach to conflict res-olution: It was fair, it was interesting, it was new. And then I pulled out the coin to flip it:

"I get to call it!"

"No, Quinn, shut up, I get to call it!"

And off they went again, at the tops of their lungs—which they will do, I now know, until Quinn clobbers Dixie with a hairbrush or Dixie rakes her fingernails across Quinn's chest or some near-mortal wound is inflicted. Earlier this very day, seeking solace, I described their strange case over lunch to a good friend who hap-pens to be a social psychologist. "Do you know the data on siblings across species?" he asked, before I was even half done. I didn't. "Oh, yeah," he said. "Half the time they kill each other." He ran through a few species: Sand-shark siblings eat each other in their mother's oviducts; hyena siblings eat each other the minute they get out. The blue-footed booby is especially ruthless: "If their siblings drop below eighty percent of normal body weight," he explained, "they peck 'em to death." That would be Dixie, whose teeth marks can now be found on her sister's legs.

I glare at my children, they glare back at me. They think I am weak, I decide. They want to play hard-ball; they don't know what hardball is. They will now learn. Yet another generous neighbor has brought us yet another extravagant dessert: a ginger and molasses cake, topped with whipped cream. But they are grounded: no desserts for a week. In better times I might sympathize with their predicament. I might toss them a crumb. At the very least I would sneak my cake later, alone. Not now. I cut myself a large piece and crown it with whipped cream, all the while feeling two pairs of eyes tracking me around the kitchen. Heaping great dollops of molasses and whipped cream onto my plate, I sit back down. Their own sad plates are decorated with cold, half-eaten vegetables.

I coat the first bite in whipped cream, swipe it once through the molasses, and, slowly, raise the fork to my mouth. Then I see Dixie's face. Her lower lip trembles and tears stream down her sweet little face. It's an involuntary response to a horrible realization: *Daddy doesn't care. He's going to inhale his yummy dessert even though he knows Dixie can't have any.* It takes a few seconds for the sobbing to kick in, as she runs from the room.

"See what you did, Daddy!" shouts Quinn, chasing after her.

Through gritted teeth I shovel the ginger and molasses cake—but as I do I sense, uneasily, that I've read this story before. I wait until everyone is asleep and then dig it out of my bookshelves. *Will This Do?* was what British journalist Auberon Waugh called his memoir. On page sixty-seven I find what I'm looking for, Auberon's description of his father, Evelyn:

> On one occasion, just after the war, the first consignment of bananas arrived. Neither I, my sister Teresa, nor my sister Margaret had ever eaten a banana but we had heard about them as the most delicious taste in the world. When this first consignment arrived the socialist government decided that every child in the country should be allowed one banana. An army of civil servants issued a library of special banana coupons, and the great day arrived when my mother came home with three bananas. All three were put on my father's plate, and before the anguished eyes of his children, he poured on cream, which was almost unprocurable, and sugar, which was heavily rationed, and ate all three.

When I first read that passage, I thought: *What a monster.* Now I think: *The poor guy.* "From then on," Auberon concluded, "I never treated anything he had to say on faith or morals very seriously." "That was the only time," I can imagine Evelyn replying, "when I treated my children with the barbarity with which they treated me."

The next morning I wake up and go to the bathroom to shower and shave. Stuck on the bathroom mirror is a dark blue Post-it. The handwriting is unmistakably Quinn's:

Meany Meany
You Are A
Meany
DAD

After that, all is silence. For the next week no one says a thing about the incident. I remove the Post-it, the girls behave better, they even get desserts. But of course no day passes without my wondering, however briefly, (a) just what damage I might have done, and (b) how the incident might play in, say, a memoir. On top of the risk that you might actually screw up your child is the risk that, even if you don't, she'll think you did and blame you for it. Finally one morning, as I drive Quinn to school, I look in the rearview mirror and ask, "You know that cake I ate when you couldn't have dessert?"

"What cake?"

"You know that note you wrote and stuck on my mirror last week?"

"What note?" she asks. I remind her, but she has

no idea what I'm talking about. Not the first clue. She doesn't even remember her sister's tears. "The problem with me," she says seriously, "is that I only remember the stuff that is a long, long time ago. I'll probably remember it in 3000."

THE LAST TIME I'd visited the fairgrounds in New Orleans was the spring of 1977, when I was sixteen years old. A classmate of mine had a gambling debt of $8,000 that he couldn't pay off—$8,000 being the equivalent today of roughly twenty-seven grand, real money for a high school junior back then. In what seemed at the time like a sensible strategy, he hocked the coin collection given to him at birth by his grandparents and came up with $2,000 cash. This he handed to me, along with instructions to go to the fairgrounds and lay it all on Albo Berry to show in the sixth. His nerves couldn't take it, he said, and besides, he had math class. Albo Berry was racing on a school day, during seventh and eighth period, when all I had was film history—which could be skipped safely. And so I grabbed another friend and drove to the fairgrounds to lay two grand on Albo Berry to show.

Probably there was some law forbidding minors from betting on horses, but it wasn't taken any more seriously than the other laws in New Orleans that separated children from the grown-up world. So long as you didn't make the enablers feel as if you were going to attract the wrong sort of attention, they let you do pretty much what you wanted. Two grand was attention-getting, however, and we decided the only safe way to get it down on Albo Berry was in small, childish chunks. The moment Albo Berry's race was announced we each took $1,000 and dashed around madly, placing $5 bets. We wound up with four hundred tickets, but we got it all down, then took a seat in the grandstand to watch the race.

They were already off; a bunch of horses had broken from the pack, Albo Berry not among them. Indeed, for the longest time Albo Berry went unmentioned. It was as if he existed only in a dream. But then, as if he knew what was at stake, he made his move. Coming hard on the outside, he passed all but two other horses. By a nose, Albo Berry showed. We spent half an hour running around collecting what came to several thousand dollars in small bills. Armloads of cash made us conspicuous, and so we made quickly for the car. Only then did a grown-up—the guard in the parking lot— take notice. We were a step too fast for him. He peered into the car window as we whizzed past, and my friend heaved all the money up into the air, so that, for that moment, the inside of the car looked like a ticker-tape parade. We made it back to school just in time for base-ball practice.

Now, for the first time in thirty years, I'm back at the

fairgrounds, with a seven-year-old daughter holding one hand and a four-year-old holding the other. I hadn't planned to teach my children how to bet on the ponies on this trip. But my brother lives down the block from the racetrack, and the three of us went to visit him for lunch, and one thing led to another. Before you could say "trifecta," we had them on our shoulders and were walking over to the races. Just one race, I told them, and then we'd leave. For old times' sake. They might learn something.

"You promise we can we bet real money?" asks Quinn.

"Yeah, Daddy," says Dixie, "can we bet real money?"

"You can each make one small bet," I say judiciously.

"You'll have to make it for us," says Quinn knowingly, " 'cause we're too little."

Through the turnstiles we plunge and make for the viewing area to decide which horse to back. But before we do, we bump into Al Stall, who'd been a year behind me in school and who has, it turns out, spent most of his time since then training racehorses. I haven't seen him since high school, but it feels like yesterday, and he ushers the kids into the space reserved for horses. He wants them to see Winsky, a sleek, tan, four-year-old mare, his horse in the race. As they inspect the animal, the jockey appears, followed by Winsky's owners, and so they inspect them, too. They listen as Al talks a little bit about his horse, the favorite. Al doesn't sound worried. Al doesn't look worried. Al, truth to tell, looks as if his horse has already won.

"I want to bet on Winsky," says Quinn firmly.

"Me, too!" says Dixie.

"If we win, you girls have to join us in the winner's circle!" says the owner.

We rush out to lay some dough on Winsky. "Daddy, what's the circle?" asks Dixie, but I'm too distracted to answer. They've replaced old tellers with new betting machines. It's now more complicated for a forty-six-year-old man to place two $5 bets on a horse to win than it was thirty years ago for a sixteen-year-old to lay two grand on a horse to show. I waste ten bucks printing out two erroneous tickets before finally getting my hands on tickets for Winsky to win. Grabbing them from me, the girls race outside to watch their horse up close, from the rail. The weather is clear, the track fast. As the bell rings and the horses bolt from the gate, I wonder: *This is what fathers are for? To take children to the places they aren't supposed to go, so that they can do the things children aren't supposed to do? If Mama's the law, I'm the blind eye.*

For roughly fifty-one weeks a year, I'm a bit player in my children's moral education. This week is the exception, when we visit New Orleans for Mardi Gras. For seven days I'm more or less in charge and use them to cultivate the aspects of their characters that they'll need to make it in the modern world: guile, greed, charm, and a deep appreciation that what you know is less important than who you know. Mardi Gras might just as well have been created to teach small children how to compete in the more ferocious sectors of our nation's economy. Beads, in the brief moment they fly through the air, become so valuable that grown men will trample one another to get them and young women will disrobe. Three hours later they're worthless again, but that's not the point. The point is how to get as many of them as possible.

Last year, when she was six, Quinn draped the beads she caught around her neck. This year she takes what she catches and squirrels it away furtively in a camouflaged Army duffel bag beside her. "If they see you have lots of loot they won't throw you anything," she explains hurriedly, and then resumes her quest for more beads. Dixie is only four, but even she seems to be coming along nicely. As I haul home a fifty-pound sack full of beads, she says, "Daddy, you want me to tell you why they gave me so many things? 'Cause I was making a sad face." Every small child in America should be flown to New Orleans for Mardi Gras. Those who excel should be offered jobs by Goldman Sachs selling bonds. Those who fail should be taken to the racetrack, to see if they are perhaps better suited to trading.

The race starts, a mile and forty yards. There is no drama to it. Winsky, on the inside, takes the lead and never surrenders it. She wins so easily that, if I were one of the other horses, I might just canter back to my stable and shoot myself. My daughters leap around: They won! "How much did we win, Daddy?" they ask but then are distracted by their new best friends, Winsky's owners, trainer, and jockey, who guide them into the winner's circle. They pose for a group photo, Quinn and Dixie front and center, as a man with a television camera races back and forth filming them from every possible angle, beaming their smiles into every off-track betting parlor in the land. Quinn sees the camera and waves.

Twenty-two minutes after they strolled into the fairgrounds, they're back in their car seats, waving $5 bills and looking for something to argue about. The experience has struck neither of them as noteworthy. The problem with lucking out with your children is that your children don't appreciate their luck—and the lucky feeling is more than half of the pleasure. You go to all this trouble to get them an education, and they promptly forget the lessons. On the drive home I explain

to them that it isn't common for two little girls to walk
into a racetrack in the middle of the day for a single
horse race and wind up in the winner's circle, holding
winning tickets, with the horse's jockey on one arm
and the horse's owner on the other. Not to mention getting serious screen time on every OTB network. It takes
some effort, but by the time we arrive home, each little
girl has been convinced she has something worth saying
about her field trip—only it isn't the same thing. Dixie,
running to the back of the house to find her mother,
squeals, "Mama, I made five dollars at the round field!"
Quinn races up the stairs, finds her grandmother, and
shouts, "Nana, we were on national TV!"

I'D DRIVEN AN hour from home to give a talk, and was up on a stage with my cell phone off, when Tabitha left three messages. In the first, she said Walker was having trouble breathing and so she was taking him to the doctor; in the second, she was on her way from the doctor's office to the emergency room; in the third, she was on the emergency-room pay phone, either crying or trying not to cry. "He has RSV," she said mysteriously, and added that he was strapped to a gurney and waiting for an ambulance to take him to a place that handled infants with RSV, whatever that was. Her cell phone wouldn't work there, she'd been told, and there was no number on which I could reach her.

And so I found myself doing eighty-five across the San Mateo Bridge, toting up in my mind how little I'd done in my son's eleven weeks on earth to keep him alive. Seventy-six nights and I'd spent zero in the same room with him, unless you counted the night of his birth, and the few times I stayed up until midnight to feed him a bottle of pumped breast milk before handing him over to his mother. Eating was another thing he'd done almost entirely without me: eight times a day, or more than six hundred daddyless meals in total. His diaper needed changing about as often as he ate, yet I'd done that seven times, and remembered each event. He slept sixteen hours a day, leaving eight in which he needed to be tended. Roughly three of those went to feeding and another to bathing and changing clothes—two more of his activities I'd managed to avoid entirely. That left him just four hours a day of what might be called discretionary leisure, or about three hundred hours total, of which I'd occupied no more than thirty.

Those were the raw stats: They shocked even me. No matter how you spun them, they suggested a truly awesome paternal neglect. (*Seven out of six hundred diapers!*) It had to be some kind of record, at least in the modern era of fatherhood. The achievement was probably in some small part due to what might be politely called an attitude problem. When asked to take the baby, even for just a few minutes, I instantly become a corporate executive sentenced to a long jail term. I race around the house cleaning up my affairs, wondering what needs to be done before I'm removed from society. But the larger part of my neglect arose from changes in the structure of our family life, brought about by the addition of a third child. Once a collectivist farm, we now had more in common with a manufacturing enterprise, beginning with a ruthlessly efficient division of labor. Mama took care of the baby; Daddy took care of everyone else, or paid other people to do it for him. Family productivity remained stable and, amazingly, Mama didn't complain about the arrangement. Many times in the past eleven weeks, I expected to be chastised for doing so little but instead found myself appreciated for doing anything at all. On those rare occasions, I was no longer a father doing his duty but an assembly line worker who has rushed down the conveyor belt to rescue a fellow worker who has fallen behind. A company hero. Worker of the month.

On this afternoon, the assembly line finally ground to a halt, its gears gummed up with paternal guilt. It took ninety minutes to get home, drop the girls with our endlessly generous neighbors, and speed back to the hospital. There I find Walker with two tubes up his nose, another in his left foot, and wires taped to his chest. Dried blood stains the blanket by his feet, where nurses have tried and failed to insert an IV drip. He looks bad, but his mother looks worse. She hasn't slept properly in months, and she's spent the last five hours watching this baby she's been caring for poked and prodded with needles and strapped down on gurneys. Four different people had offered her four different explanations of RSV, but the hardest piece of information she'd come away with was that she should expect Walker to be in the hospital for at least a week. "Don't worry," she says, reading my mind. "I'll spend the nights with him."

Thirty minutes later the door closes behind her, and she's gone. It's just him and me, for the first time, really. Except for his sad little wheezing sounds and the beeping of the machine that measures the amount of oxygen in his blood, the room is silent.

RSV, it turns out, stands for respiratory syncytial virus. From the point of view of Berkeley's infants, it might as well be the bubonic plague. The hospital floor has twenty-eight beds, and twenty-five of them are occupied by infants with RSV, who share one other trait in common: older siblings in school. School-aged children are the rats of our time. After a day of happily swapping germs with their peers, my children apparently returned home with what probably felt to them like a mild cold, and kissed their baby brother—who promptly lost his ability to breathe. There's little that medicine can do for him except attach him to a machine that measures the oxygen in his blood, and, if he's about to suffocate, attach him to an artificial respirator.

My job as his attendant is to decide when he's about to suffocate. Over his bed is a black box that blinks bright red digits, like a radar gun. One hundred is a perfect score. Under ninety and the box starts to beep, and I'm meant to call a nurse to suction the mucus from his nose and mouth. For an hour or so, his number is a reassuring ninety-four, but then it plummets, and I call a nurse. Twenty minutes later it happens again, and then again and again. It's about six at night when at length he is finally able to breathe properly, and falls asleep. That's when the phone rings. I didn't even know there was a phone, but there it is, howling, right beside his ear. He wakes up and begins to cry. I pick it up. It's a woman who says she's from the hospital's "financial counseling department." The department has checked our health insurance, she says, and discovered that we have a hundred-dollar deductible.

"So?" I say. Walker's now trying to holler. Only he has no voice, so the cries emerge as tiny gasps.

"How do you want to pay?" she asks.

"Just send it to me," I say.

"We typically collect before you leave the hospital," she says.

"Can't you just stick it in the mail?" I ask.

"I'll send over by courier," she says.

Forty minutes later the patient is soothed and sleeping again when in charges a nurse. "Where's Mama?" she asks loudly. Walker wakes up and begins to cry. The nurse tsk-tsks around him until he is inconsolable and

then finally says, "There should be more fathers like
you." "There are!" I want to say, but before I can, she's
gone, and I'm working to get him back to sleep.

Thirty minutes later the courier bangs on the door,
with the bill, waking him all over again. And so it goes,
for the next twenty-four hours. Bill collectors, nurses,
doctors, interns, floor cleaners, linen changers: As soon
as he's recovered from one of their visits and fallen back
to sleep, another bursts into the room and disturbs him
all over again. Each time he wakes, he cries, and each
time he cries, he generates mucus, and each time he
generates mucus, he begins to wheeze and his radar-gun
readings plummet. The odd thing about this is that the
doctors all admit *that there is nothing they can do for him.*
He's in the hospital only so he can be near an artificial
respirator. But the hospital seems only to increase the
likelihood that he'll need an artificial respirator. Such
is the state of our health-care system: They keep you
from dying, but somehow leave you feeling you're getting the raw end of the deal. Asking politely for peace
and quiet does no good; the nurses change every four
minutes, and the new one never has any idea what the
old one did or didn't do. After the fifteenth time he's
awakened, I decide that it's time for a show of paternal
authority. I make a sign:

PLEASE DO NOT DISTURB.
I'M SLEEPING.
THANK YOU.
WALKER.

I tape it to one side of the door, and drag the chair that doubles as a bed against the other, so that no one can enter without climbing over it, and me. Then I hunker down, like some Montana survivalist, and wait for the enemy. The first assault comes about ten o'clock that night: a new nurse.

"Can I help you?" I say curtly.

"I just want to look at him."

"Why?"

"We're supposed to," she says—which is to say that even she knows she serves no good purpose other than to collect evidence for any future lawsuit.

"Nope," I say.

And she leaves!

I repel several more assaults until, finally, word must have spread that there's a total asshole guarding the little boy in Room 5426, because we find ourselves well and truly alone. I change his diapers and feed him and suction the mucus from his nose. I notice for the first time that he has my hands and feet. I study the little heart-shaped birthmark on the back of his head. I discover that if I hold him to my chest and hum against the back of his neck, he falls right to sleep. Tabitha comes and offers to take over, but the truth is I don't want to leave: He feels like my jurisdiction. After every new child, I learn the same lesson, grudgingly: If you want to feel the way you're meant to feel about the new baby, you need to do the grunt work. It's only in caring for a thing that you become attached to it.

And he gets better, and better. On the third day, he's hitting one hundred on the radar gun, and seems almost himself. At six o'clock that morning, an intern—a student who is there for no reason other than to satisfy his curiosity—catches me off guard in the bathroom. But I hear a stir. I bound out to discover this child-doctor bent over my son, preparing to apply cold metal to sleeping flesh.

"What do you think you're doing?" I snap at him.

"Can I listen to his breathing?" he asks. He's not even a doctor. He's a tourist.

"No!" I boom, Shrek-like. I haven't slept in two days and I'm in no mood. Still, it comes out a more menacing sound than I intended. The poor kid actually trots out the door. Then I look down at Walker and, unless I'm mistaken, he's laughing. He's got tubes coming out of every orifice, and he's having a ball. We're just two guys in a foxhole, defending ourselves against repeated, ceaseless assaults from the hospital staff.

"How you doin', buddy?" I say.

"Coo!" he says, and smiles. It's a big sloppy grin. It's then that the doctor arrives, with good news. She points to the black box over his head—his number flashes between ninety-four and ninety-six—and says, "He's the strongest on the floor." My first thought: *There are twenty-four other kids with the same thing and they're all more likely to die than he is, and . . . since no one ever heard of twenty-five kids dying in a children's hospital . . . he's not going to die.* My second thought: *He's winning the RSV tourney!* I look down at him, proudly. He smiles again. I'm hooked.

SPLAYED ON THE operating table, staring at the back of a nurse scrubbing her hands, I was struck by the possibility that, in addition to its other challenges, a vasectomy might be a socially awkward experience. "Do you need to empty your bladder?" asked the nurse, who clearly found hospital English the safest language in which to address a stranger's genitals. The clinic walls were undecorated, save for a lone medical drawing of the male sex organ, flayed to reveal its sober inner logic.

"I don't think so," I said.

"Okay," she said. "I'll be right back to give you a shaving," and left to do whatever nurses do before they apply razors to testicles. Two months earlier, in the pre-interview, during which it was determined that whatever I may have been told by my wife or the state police, I was under no legal obligation to be sterilized, the doctor explained that California law required a cooling-off period between consultation and operation. On that chilly afternoon, he told me many other things about vasectomies but somehow failed to mention that they began with a good ball-shaving from a woman who didn't look you in the eye, or say a word beyond the bare minimum.

The nurse returned, wearing the same blank expression but now waving a new disposable razor, which struck me as a cheap tool for a dear job. She worked quickly and joylessly, like a Marine barber. I wanted to be helpful but there wasn't much to do, except to hope she didn't flinch. In the vast silence, insane thoughts flitted across my disturbed mind.

Is it possible to shave something off by mistake?

Jesus Christ . . . What if I get an erection?

Would it be my last?

Maybe I should pop one off, just for old times' sake.

There are times when the mind is a dangerous place to be, and this was one of them. The ceiling, like the floor, was speckled linoleum. I stopped thinking and counted speckles until, at length, she finished. Chucking the disposable razor, she said, "The doctor will be here in twenty minutes."

The interesting thing about twenty minutes is how many more they can seem to be. One of the reasons I found myself on this table was that I hadn't imagined what exactly was going to be done here. I now had time to consider the matter and ask myself a few obvious questions. For example: *What the hell am I doing here?* In theory, the answer was at hand. My wife wanted me to be here, and it seemed too transparently selfish to refuse. She'd endured three pregnancies, suffered the pain and indignity of three childbirths, changed most of the diapers, gotten up most of the mornings, and, on top of it all, given me the leisure to keep a journal of complaints about the inconveniences of fatherhood. The time had come for Daddy to take one for the team.

This explanation had sufficed—right up to this moment. Now, with the doctor's scalpel just minutes away, it was drowned out by a new sound, of a grown man screaming:

THEY'RE GOING TO CUT A HOLE IN MY JOHNSON!

I mean, why am I really here, stretched out and hairless and exposed and not knowing what to say to the mute lady scraping away south of the border? I now asked myself. *What's the meaning of this outrage?* This operation wasn't about birth control. It was about life control. I should have fought for my reproductive rights, like other men. A friend of mine, when his wife suggested he might go and get himself gelded, had just laughed and said, "What if I want a trophy wife one day?" Another had declined his wife's invitation to a beheading by saying, "What if you and the kids go down in a plane crash?" Other men I knew refused on the grounds of rumors they'd heard about the operation's side effects. "I have a friend who had it done and he couldn't feel his dick for *ten months*," a guy at a dinner party told me knowledgeably. "After that I said, 'No way.' "

And these were men who lived in *Berkeley, California*! Imagine the conversation in the red states, where men were men. One day someone is going to interview a statistically representative cross section of the population and write the definitive sociological treatise on the hidden debate inside the post-reproductive American marriage about whose loins were meant to be surgically closed for business. As that treatise has not yet been written, we are left to guess at its future conclusions. My own guess is that wives across America are seeking, OPEC-like, to control the flow of their husbands' sperm while those husbands are struggling to keep the pipelines open. There's a war being waged for control over a precious resource, but without correspondents. The only news comes from couples in which the male already has been neutered: These people of course always piously claim that it was never really an issue and the husband honestly never wanted anything so much as to become an It.

Alone on the operating table, I got myself well and truly worked up. Then, from nowhere came another voice. "You're being a dick," it said.

Sweet Reason had intervened. "You are not being fair," she said. "You agreed to do this and she never really pressed you that hard, except to remind you every two months that you had promised to do it, and to ask if you had scheduled the appointment." I began to list all the good things I could think of about being sterile:

1. If my wife gets pregnant, I'll know for sure that I am not the father.
2. If some other woman gets pregnant, I can't convincingly be blamed for it.

Maybe it was my inability to think up a third item for the list, or perhaps it was the bright red flayed penis on the wall beside me, but now a new notion popped into my head: *Flee!* Shaved goolies and all, I could leap off the table before the doctor arrived. My car was a mere forty yards away. Forty yards I could still dash, intact. A Man In Full. To seem heroic, while at the same time maximizing sympathy for myself afterward, I'd driven myself to the doctor's office and was driving myself home. No one would ever know.

The doctor entered.

He raised my dressing gown, took a perfunctory let's-see-what-we-have-here peek. We exchanged pleasantries. If he had any sense of the mental turmoil he'd interrupted, he hid it well. "There's something I've been wondering about," I said. "But you have to promise me, if I ask, you will tell me the truth."

"I promise," he said.

"Have you ever opened that door thinking there was a patient in here and found no one on this table?"

He laughed. "You mean does anyone ever chicken out?"

"Yes."

"No. Not once," he said. "But it's funny. About one in four—no, maybe more like one in three—schedule the operation and never show up."

Yes, I agreed, that was a riot. Then it wasn't: There was a needle in my scrotum. Scrotums were not designed with needles in mind. But this doctor worked quickly. So quickly, in fact, that I couldn't help but suspect he knew he must work quickly, or find himself chasing down the highway after his patients. My hands were now clenched and tearing at the sanitary paper bedspread. "It'll only sting for a minute," he said. "After this, if you experience any really sharp pain, you should tell me."

But there was no more sharp pain: For the next thirty minutes, I felt instead a strange pulling and pinching, along with an occasional heavy stomach wrenching sensation, as if he were seeing, just for fun, what would happen if you applied 170 pounds of pressure on a single male testicle. A vasectomy feels half the time as if you are being kneaded into a loaf of bread and the other half of the time as if you are being sewn into a quilt.

And that is the spirit in which the doctor worked: of a man either baking or knitting. He chatted as he sewed, or baked as he chatted, and after a stretch I realized that I'd become so wholly focused on being ready to shriek at the top of my lungs at the first sharp pain that I had failed to keep up my end of the conversation.

"Tell me something else," I said, interrupting whatever he was saying.

"What's that?"

"Do you have children?" I asked.

"Yes."

"Do you intend to have more?"

"No."

"Have you had this done to yourself?"

"No," he said, with a slight pause. "I haven't."

"Hypocrite."

He laughed. "You don't know the details," he said. But he was done, and so were we. "Okay, you can get dressed," he said. "But be careful." He left the room. I rose from the table, and wobbled. Glued by sweat to my backside, from neck to thigh, was a paper bedsheet that came away only in strips and patches as I picked at it. I stepped into my pants, hobbled to my car, and drove myself home. A hero to my wife. A traitor to my sex. A thoroughly modern American guy.

EVERY NIGHT AFTER Walker is asleep and the girls are in their bunk bed, Tabitha reads to Quinn from a book about puberty. This might seem premature—she only just turned nine—but it's breathtakingly shrewd. If you introduce the general concepts to a child early enough you might screw them up for life, but you also catch them before they know enough to be embarrassed or to make you squirm. Sprouting hair, sprouting body parts, foul body odors, gooey emissions—all are facts to be absorbed, and even things to be hoped for. Every morning as they brush their teeth, Quinn gives Dixie a powerful lecture on who gets hair where and when; and who smells badly in which place and why. Neither professor nor pupil giggles or squirms or exhibits so much as a trace of self-consciousness. This knowledge transfer is not at all as I remember it; it's all so grown-up and even un-American; they might as well be French. Yesterday Quinn insisted on being taken to buy brassieres. Seeing the flat, cupless pile, Dixie asked seriously, "Did Quinn catch puberty?"

From her position on the bottom bunk Dixie has learned enough to feel left out. When I come to read to her she reaches for a book called *Mommy Laid an Egg*. *Mommy Laid an Egg* is a cartoon to explain to small children where babies come from, so their parents never have to. In *Mommy Laid an Egg*, Daddy has pods, and Mommy has a pod receptacle. Daddy inserts pods into Mommy's pod receptacle and a baby grows. But *Mommy Laid an Egg* goes further, for it shows Mommy receiving Daddy's pods not just gleefully, but with reckless abandon, eighteen different ways from Sunday. It shows pictures of Mommy and Daddy humping away on a skateboard, for instance, and other pictures of Mommy and Daddy banging away on the kitchen counter. It's a little shocking and at the same time reassuring that this sort of thing can still get past the censors. After all, they removed the ashtray from *Goodnight Moon*.

At any rate, none of this seems to have the slightest effect on Dixie. Instead she dwells, at length, on the cartoon of the birth itself. It shows the stick-figure baby emerging from a stick-figure Mommy, but because they are nothing but stick figures the path of exit remains a little hazy.

"I'm not going to have any babies," she says finally.

"Why not?" asks Tabitha from above.

"I don't want anything coming out of my butthole," says Dixie, and yawns.

"It doesn't come out of your butthole," says Quinn knowingly—but then, she now says everything knowingly. "It comes out your VULVA."

Dixie's falling asleep and Quinn is just starting a new chapter on body odor, which is apparently so gripping that she will spend the next few days convinced that she has it. I leave them to it, but the moment I'm gone Quinn turns to Tabitha and asks, "Why did Daddy have a bisectomy?"

"It's called a vasectomy," says Tabitha.

"No, it's not," says Quinn

"What's a bisectomy?" asks Dixie.

"A VAS-ectomy," says Tabitha wearily.

"Yeah," says Quinn, "but the reason Daddy's pods don't work anymore is because he had a BI-sectomy."

Alas, Daddy's pods do not lend themselves to such definitive statements. As the surgeon who'd done the job explained, a vasectomy doesn't end anything. It merely cuts off the new supply of live sperm; there's apparently a holding tank teeming with the reckless critters that needs to be emptied, and emptying it can take—well, that depends. A friend fresh from the operating table was told by his doctor he needed to have sex six times before he even bothered being tested for sterility and he burst out, "That's a whole year!" My own doctor had skipped the small talk and told me to wait six months, then go into a lab and take a semen test.

That was seven months ago. For seven months I've had this scene playing in the back of my mind: face to face with a perfect stranger, I need to explain to him—but probably her—that I've come to produce, and to hand over, my sperm. What happens next? How does this conversation play out? I wasn't sure except it was clear that the easy way out—generating the specimen in the comfort and privacy of one's home—wasn't an option, unless one was prepared to pack it just so into an ice chest and race it over to the lab within the hour. Home manufacture wasn't recommended. So how, exactly, did this business work?

As it happened I was scheduled for a checkup with my regular doctor, and so used it as an excuse to wait and hear what he had to say about it. "I had that vasectomy we talked about!" I said cheerfully as he took my blood pressure.

"How did it go?"

"Hard to say," I said. Then, as casually as possible, "How do they collect that sperm sample anyway?"

"You just go to the lab and they give you a cup," he said.

"Just like that?"

"Just like that."

"They don't do anything to—uh—help you out?"

"You mean do they provide you with a woman?" he exclaimed, with a great heaving guffaw, loudly enough to be heard up and down the hallway.

"No, of course not!"

"Then what do you mean?" he asked.

I obviously didn't want to say what I meant. What I meant was that no one could really be expected to walk into some office and tell a complete stranger that he needed not only a place to jerk off, but a cup to do it in. There are limits, even in America, even in 2008. I assumed there had to be a less conspicuous way to handle this problem.

"It just strikes me as a little socially awkward," I said.

"Here," he said—and he wrote out a request for a blood test. "Just take this in and have the semen work done the same time as the blood work."

And so it is that I find myself pedaling my mountain bike over to the nearest offices of Quest Diagnostics, next door to the hospital where all of my children were born. My sweaty palms clutch two forms, one for the blood (the cover), the other for the sperm (the mission). It'll be quick, I tell myself, like a shot. People do it every day. There must be some obvious protocol.

There isn't. What there is, instead, is a small room full of women. Most of them sit at a safe distance in chairs ringing the room, reading three-month-old copies of *People* magazine, but a few linger around the front desk. The front desk offers no private space; it's just a desk, with another woman behind it. And not a reassuringly sexless battleship of a woman; a shapely and pretty woman, who looks as if she might never have been on the receiving end of a sperm sample. Worse, the women closest to her desk are not waiting their turn but just waiting. Loitering. Seeing what's up.

"Can I help you?" asks the pretty young woman behind the desk.

I can hear the rustling of *People*s; I can feel the ladies behind me taking an interest in my case. Already I'm sweating from the bike ride. I also have failed to remove my bicycle helmet. I resemble, perhaps, a bike messenger. With a special delivery.

"I need a blood test," I say casually. I hand her the form and, as I do, imagine the ladies behind me losing interest. Then, as the lady behind the desk looks over the blood work form, I say quickly, "Also this." I push across the doctor's formal request for the scoop on my semen. She looks it over, and motions to a room behind her. "In there for the blood test," she says discreetly. "For the other you'll need this." She hands me a plastic cup and a leaflet. "You don't do that here. You take it over to our office around the corner."

I'd underestimated her. She was clearly an old pro at this. In a stroke she made it easier than I'd ever hoped. No titters; no meaningful eye contact; no embarrassing words—words like "sperm" or "masturbate." I wasn't marched off before a crowd into some public chicken chokin' chamber in which I would be compelled to produce my own seed while strangers with X-ray vision swarmed outside. Everything was on the leaflet, in more or less these words:

PUT SAMPLE IN CUP.

DROP CUP AT OTHER OFFICE WHERE NO ONE KNOWS YOU OR WILL EVER SEE YOU AGAIN.

NO NEED TO DISCUSS DETAILS.

I gave blood with gusto, then, little cup in hand, marched out into the street and back onto my bike. Only then did it strike me that there was a single unresolved issue: how to get the sample into the cup. Surely that question would answer itself at the second office. The kind and thoughtful and sensitive people of Quest Diagnostics had thought of everything; they, like I, wanted only to minimize the intimacy of our dealings. There'd be some . . . private place. But then I arrive at the second office.

This second office has much in common with the first—more old copies of *People* magazine, more strange women, another stranger behind another desk—but lacks something the other had: a bathroom. I cast in vain around the ground floor of the six-story building, then waste ten minutes riding the elevator in search of a private bathroom. At every floor I get off and march the halls. These other floors indeed have bathrooms, but they're locked and reserved for patients of the various doctors. Each door I yank more frantically than the last, but none so much as budge. I consider opening one of the dark wooden doors to a doctor's private offices and asking for a key, but think better of it. I'm not a patient. People might ask questions.

Now I'm back out on the street, back on my bike, plastic cup in hand. No way I'm going back to the first office with the sad little cup and asking the pretty woman behind the desk to use her bathroom: that would be mortifying and might even violate the Quest Diagnostic rules. I'm handling this myself. Around and around the neighborhood I cycle, scouting locations. The streets of Berkeley were built to accommodate many interest groups—pedestrians, wheelchair riders, cyclists—but apparently no one gave a thought to my perverse own.

Then I spot the parking garage.

It's full; the sign says so. Full is good: no one is going to stumble in looking for a place to park. With no one entering, the only risk is someone exiting—but it's the middle of the afternoon and the doctors and nurses who have no doubt parked here are still working. It's dark and peaceful and quiet as a graveyard. I find an especially large SUV and wheel my bike between its front bumper and a concrete wall. Only then does it occur to me:

YOU ARE ABOUT TO WHACK OFF INTO A SMALL PLAS-TIC CUP IN A PUBLIC PARKING GARAGE.

This thought was quickly followed by another:

YOU'RE GOING TO GET CAUGHT.

There are those, I am aware, who would find this thought erotic. Happily, I am not among them. This wasn't going to happen. I cycled back to the first building, where I'd noticed there was an unattended lobby where I could sit and think things over. For the next ten minutes I sat on the green leatherette sofa beside an elderly woman who appeared to be blind. Neither of us said a word. A Google search of the matter had revealed that some huge percentage of men who undergo vasectomies never bother to show up for a test to determine if the thing was a success. We know our strengths. We don't do well in these situations.

At length a hospital maintenance person passes through the lobby. Dangling from his belt appear to be about sixty-five keys. He walks purposefully down the long hall, and, after fiddling for many seconds to find the right key, opens a door. I race down the hall after him and put my ear to the unmarked door. Nasty bathroom sounds! There, outside, I wait, for three, four, then five minutes. Finally, with a flush and a roar, he emerges.

"You want to use it?" he asks.

"I do."

"It's supposed to be for staff," he says.

"That's okay," I say.

"Take your chances," he says, and lets me enter the cold, cramped, tiled room. It has the charm of a new mausoleum. The odor, too. I lock the door behind me and stare at the ceiling. Self-abuse: never was that term of art more apt.

Twenty minutes later, I cycle back to the second Quest Diagnostics office, toss the sad little cup at a jolly man behind the counter, and flee.

A week later I receive an e-mail from my regular doctor. "The blood test came out great," he writes. "Congratulations." Another week passes, then another, but I fail to hear from the surgeon who performed the vasectomy. Finally, I pick up the phone and, feeling a bit as though I'm calling Harvard after the acceptances have been sent out to find out why I haven't received mine, call him. The woman on the other end of the line, like all his office staff, is Chinese. Her English is broken.

"What your name?" she asks.

"Lewis."

"Lewis. You wait minute."

I wait a minute. I hear rustling, confusion, a muffled conversation.

"Lewis?"

"Yes?"

"You have live sperm!"

I think: *She's speaking a language not her own.* But no matter how I reprocess the sentence, I can't turn it into "Your operation was a success."

"What does that mean?" I ask.

"I just tell you! You have live sperm! You have live sperm!"

"Yes, but what does that *mean*?" I ask.

"Use protection!"

"Are you saying that the operation didn't work?"

I could almost hear her thinking what she'd been told to say, and not say. "Well," she finally says, "operation not working now!"

"Can I speak to the doctor?"

"Doctor with patient."

"I need to talk to him."

"He with patient!"

"I need to talk to him."

"You want doctor to call you?"

I did. And he didn't, for hours. In those hours I came privately to terms with what had just happened. A terrible practical joke. A botched execution. A crime against humanity. Alone and entirely pathetic, I moped around my office and then set off on the day's errands.

I'd done my bit. I'd found the leading sperm killer in a twenty-mile radius—the guy had shuttered some of the leading inseminators of the Bay Area. If the sperm of Northern California ever organized themselves into a fighting force, they'd lay siege to his office and run him on a rail out of the state. I'd shown up for the operation, resisted the temptation to flee the table, sweated through a hospital gown, sat around for days on bags of frozen peas, and then, after the scars healed, mourned in silence the death of my reproductive powers. That those powers still roamed the earth wasn't my fault. Or was it?

Was it possible that some sperm were simply invincible? So relentless . . . so *determined* . . . that no mere vasectomy was ever going to vanquish them? Just to ask the question was to answer it. By the time I pulled into the Best Buy parking lot I was almost giddy. Nature had created an impossible situation; this thing was out of my or anyone else's control. This fire would have to burn itself out naturally.

About then my cell phone rang. Standing between the Best Buy customer service counter and the shelf displaying the new Hewlett-Packard desktop computers, I looked down and saw that the good doctor was finally calling me back. I answered, and set out to explain how I was coming to terms with my sperm's invincibility, when he cut me off.

"Here's the thing," he said. "They send us back this form and there's a box that says 'between zero and one sperm.' That's the box they checked. But what does that mean? How can there be between zero and one sperm?"

"You tell me."

"They found one sperm. It could have been one that had been attached to a tube and got knocked off when you produced the sample. Who knows?"

"But it says I have live sperm."

"It says you had one sperm."

One heroic sperm. This one final sperm had gone by itself into the death-dealer's lab at Quest Diagnostics. It had fought the battle, so that others might live. I should hunt it down and give it a proper burial.

"The typical sample has twenty million live sperm in it."

"But if there's one there must be more, right?"

"Look," he says, "who knows where that one came from? The bottom line is that you're not going to get anyone pregnant ever again."

I think about this.

"You can come in to talk about it if you want," he says kindly.

Oddly enough, I don't.

But that night I have a dream. I dream that Nicholas Lemann, dean of the Columbia School of Journalism, is the starting point guard for the New York Knicks. In this dream, the entire New York Knicks team, bench players included, lay slumbering in a giant bed beside me, when an old girlfriend of mine storms into the room and wakes me up. The old girlfriend doesn't resemble her old self, however, but appears in the guise of a large, hairy rat. Most of the dream involves wrestling her out of the room, avoiding her many attempts to lick me with her wet, sloppy rat-tongue, and preventing her from waking up the Knicks, who have a big game the next day.

All of which is a backhanded tribute to the sheer

power of the sleeping pills they give new mothers with severe panic disorder. These pills are all that remain of Tabitha's postpartum panic attacks and they've been a godsend, not just to her but also to me: They'd put an elephant to sleep. Eager for what looked as if it might be a well-earned rest, I'd popped one of them—moments later Nick Lemann was dishing out assists and jacking up three-point shots.

And the only reason I remember any of it is that I'm awakened before it ends, by a small child standing beside my bed. Every few months one or the other of the girls shows up in our bedroom in the middle of the night—bright-eyed, sneaky smiles—to announce she's having a nightmare. Tonight, I see, we have Dixie.

"Daddy, I had a bad dream," she says.

My mind is having trouble making the transition from my own weird space to hers. What was the point of that giant hairy rat? And the Knicks? Maybe after this strange and unsettling day I needed some professional athletes around as symbols of manhood—but then surely I would have picked the Celtics, or even the Hornets. Then I remember: It was Nick Lemann who said I shouldn't write about my kids, especially as they grew older, because I'd screw them up. Nick's usually right about everything, so he's probably right about this, too. Has the time come, perhaps, to stop writing about them? If so, what will I have to look back on at the end of it?

Like dreams, these fatherhood moments are easily forgotten and no doubt also a lot more interesting to the teller than to anyone else. But when they're forgotten, their lessons, such as they are, are lost. The vacuum winds up being filled by experts on child rearing, and books on fatherhood, and social counselors and psychiatrists—the outside world has a lot to tell you about how to be a father and how to raise your children, and its advice no doubt serves some purpose. It fails, however, to get across with sufficient clarity the final rule of fatherhood: If you're not bothered by it, or disturbed by it, or messed up from it, you're probably doing something wrong that will mess up your kids. You're probably doing something wrong anyway, but that's okay: You can only do so much to mess up your kids. They can always get back at you, in therapy or their memoirs. But if you don't monitor these small creatures closely, they have the power to screw you up forever. So watch out for yourself—but don't let anyone know that's what you're doing.

I'm still staring into the shadow of a six-year-old. "What did you dream?" I say, dragging Dixie into our bed, and noting that the digital clock reads 3:22.

"I dreamed I was all alone," she says.

"How'd that make you feel?"

"Sad. I was crying. Real crying."

With that she scrambles gleefully up and into the space between mother and father, and proves again that a California king-sized bed is so big that it can comfortably sleep three adults or one six-year-old child.

ACKNOWLEDGMENTS

Much of this book appeared over the last eight years as part of a peripatetic series in *Slate*, the Web magazine founded by Michael Kinsley—Quinn's godfather—and subsequently edited by Jacob Weisberg. Jacob has children the same ages as my first two, and if he's never matched my self-pity he has often encouraged it. Al Zuckerman, who has represented me ably for many years, came up with the idea of expanding the things I'd written for *Slate* into a book. The first reaction of many readers to the original series was to pity the woman who was married to its author. Her name is Tabitha Soren, and I do, at times, pity her. Mainly I'm grateful to her, however. She served as editor, fact-checker, and, of course, incubator of the source material.